Welcome to ALL YOU **Real Family Food**, the perfect answer to that everyday question: "What's for dinner?" If you're like us, you love to flip through cookbooks— for inspiration, for ideas, for fun—and we think this one will soon become one of your favorites. To make cooking for your family quick and easy, we've collected our favorite recipes from past issues of ALL YOU in one volume, illustrated it with mouth-watering photography and added plenty of tips and hints that will make your time in the kitchen simpler and more pleasurable.

Made with ingredients that are easy to find, and written with ALL YOU's clear, concise directions, these dishes will take you through the year. Hearty recipes like **Pasta and Bean Soup with Cheese Toasts** (page 47) will help take the chill out of the winter months; simple and delicious dishes such as **Bacon and Tomato Pasta Salad** (page 50) are perfect for summertime when you can't bear to turn on your oven; you will enjoy spring's bounty with **Rhubarb and Strawberry Crisp** (page 82); and **Lots o' Lemon Meringue Pie** (page 78) is perfect for the summer and, well, anytime!

At ALL YOU, we're dedicated to giving readers everything they need to make life easier. We know that many of you do your best to eat healthfully, so we've included nutritional information for each recipe. We also know that balancing the family budget is important, so we've also added an easy-to-follow "cost per serving" rating for each recipe, so you can create great-value midweek meals, and spend a little more on celebrations and treats:

¢	each serving costs less than $1
$	each serving costs between $1 to $1.99
$$	each serving costs between $2 to $2.99
$$$	each serving costs between $3 to $3.99
$$$$	each serving cost $4 or more.

ALL YOU's aim is to make your life simpler and more enjoyable every single day. We hope that **Real Family Food** will be another way we can help you reach that goal.

Sincerely,

Isobel McKenzie-Price

Editor In Chief Isobel McKenzie-Price
Creative Director Sara Pates
Art Production Manager Jamie Roth

President Andy Blau
Publisher Diane Oshin
Account Manager Tim Hall
Consumer Marketing Director Gary Foodim

Publisher Richard Fraiman
Executive Director, Marketing Services Carol Pittard
Director, Retail & Special Sales Tom Mifsud
Marketing Director, Branded Businesses Swati Rao
Director, New Product Development Peter Harper
Financial Director Steven Sandonato
Assistant General Counsel Dasha Smith Dwin
Marketing Manager Victoria Alfonso
Book Production Manager Suzanne Janso
Design and Prepress Manager Anne-Michelle Gallero

Special thanks Bozena Bannett, Alexandra Bliss, Glenn
Buonocore, Robert Marasco, Brooke McGuire, Jonathan
Polsky, Chavaughn Raines, Mary Sarro-Waite, Ilene
Schreider, Adriana Tierno

© Copyright 2006
Time Inc. Home Entertainment

Published by ALL YOU Books
Time Inc.
1271 Avenue of the Americas
New York, New York 10020

ISBN 13: 978-1-933821-27-6
ISBN 10: 1-933821-27-2

We welcome your comments and suggestions
about ALL YOU Books. Please write to us at:
ALL YOU Books
Attention: Book Editors
P.O. Box 11016
Des Moines, IA 50336-1016

If you would like to order any of our hardcover Collector's
Edition books, please call us at 1-800-327-6388 (Monday
through Friday, 7:00 a.m.–8:00 p.m. or Saturday, 7:00
a.m.–6:00 p.m. Central Time).

DOWNTOWN BOOKWORKS INC.

President Julie Merberg
Project Editor Sara Newberry
Design Joel Avirom, Jason Snyder, Meghan Day
Healey

Special thanks Pam Abrams, Patty Brown, Dinah
Dunn, Sarah Parvis

Notice: The recipes in this book are to be followed
exactly as written. No party involved in the
production of this book is responsible for your specific
health or allergy needs that may require
medical supervision, or for any adverse reactions to
the recipes contained in this book.

Pretty-in-Pink Strawberry Cake page 88

Apple and Beet Salad page 12

Tennessee Buttermilk Biscuits page 71

Peanut Butter–Chocolate Cookie Ice Cream Cake page 81

Spaghetti and Easy Meatballs page 43

Crispy Baked Chicken page 21

Peach and Blackberry Crumble   page 83

Bacon and Tomato Pasta Salad   page 50

Contents

Cheese and Tomato Toasts   page 8

Spinach and Avocado Salad   page 11

Quick Crab Cocktail   page 14

Creamy Ginger-Parsnip Soup page 15

Appetizers

In this chapter, we offer 12 fabulous recipes for perfect beginnings to meals. From elegant starters such as **Shrimp Cocktail on Skewers** (page 9) to easy and delicious dips like **Quick Crab Cocktail** (page 14), we've got your party prep covered.

And for those times when you'd like a little something extra to start a meal (or are in the mood for a lighter main dish), we've got satisfying and flavorful choices like **Apple and Beet Salad** (page 12) and **Roasted Red Pepper Soup** (page 16).

THE EASIEST APPETIZERS

If you're really pressed for time, try one of these fast-and-easy starters:

Baked Brie: Wrap a round of Brie cheese in a rolled out sheet of puff pastry. Brush pastry with 1 egg yolk stirred together with 1 tsp. water. Bake at 450°F for 20 minutes, until pastry is golden.

Tuscan White Bean Spread: Drain a can of white beans and cook them with olive oil and crushed garlic, then mash well. Serve as a dip with slices of crusty bread.

Asparagus Soup: Sauté 1 chopped onion in butter, then sprinkle with 1 Tbsp. flour. Stir in 2 cans chicken broth and bring to a boil. Add 1 lb. asparagus, cut into 1-inch pieces and cook for 25 minutes. Drain, reserving liquid. Puree asparagus, then stir purée into liquid and season with salt to taste.

Guacamole page 14

Shrimp Cocktail on Skewers

PREP: 20 min.   COOK: 2 min.   SERVES: 8   COST PER SERVING: $

- 24 large shrimp (about 1 lb.) in their shells
- 1 cup bottled cocktail sauce
- 2 tsp. fresh lime juice
- 2 tsp. minced jalapeño
- 24 (9-inch) wooden skewers
- Limes, cut in half, for serving

1 In a large pot of boiling salted water, cook shrimp until they're bright pink and opaque throughout, 2 minutes. Drain and refresh under cold water to stop cooking; pat dry. Remove shells, leaving tails on for serving, if desired. Refrigerate, tightly wrapped, until ready to serve. (Shrimp may be cooked up to 1 day ahead.)

2 Stir together cocktail sauce, lime juice and jalapeño in a small serving bowl until well combined. Cover and refrigerate until ready to serve. (Sauce may be prepared up to 1 day ahead.)

3 Thread each shrimp on a bamboo skewer and stand up in a clear pitcher lined with cut limes. Serve with cocktail sauce.

PER SERVING: Cal. 91, Fat 1g (Sat. 0g), Chol. 86mg, Fiber 1g, Pro. 12g, Carb. 8g, Sod. 424mg

Cheese and Tomato Toasts

PREP: 15 min.   COOK: 5 min.   SERVES: 8   COST PER SERVING: $

- 5 to 6 oz. mild, creamy goat cheese or cream cheese, at room temperature
- 2 Tbsp. chopped parsley
- ¼ tsp. ground black pepper
- 2 plum tomatoes, seeded and diced
- 3 Tbsp. olive oil
- ⅛ tsp. salt
- 1 loaf (about 8 oz.) Italian bread
- 2 cloves garlic, halved

1 Preheat oven to 400°F. Stir together goat cheese, 1 Tbsp. parsley and pepper in a small bowl until thoroughly combined. Stir together tomatoes, 2 tsp. olive oil, salt and 1½ tsp. parsley in a medium bowl.

2 Slice off and discard ends of bread. Slice loaf diagonally into ½-inch-thick slices and place on a baking sheet. Toast in oven until golden brown, about 5 minutes. Rub 1 side of each toast slice with cut side of garlic, then brush the same side with remaining olive oil.

3 Just before serving, spread toast slices with cheese mixture and top with tomato mixture. Sprinkle remaining 1½ tsp. parsley on top.

PER SERVING: Cal. 173, Fat 10g (Sat. 4g), Chol. 8mg, Fiber 1g, Pro. 6g, Carb. 15g, Sod. 262mg

Greek Salad

PREP: 10 min. SERVES: 4 COST PER SERVING: $$$

- 6 small ripe tomatoes, cut into wedges
- 1 small European cucumber (about 10 oz.), peeled and sliced ¼ inch thick
- 1 small red onion, thinly sliced into rings
- 3 Tbsp. extra-virgin olive oil
- 1 Tbsp. red wine vinegar
- 2 Tbsp. chopped fresh parsley
- ¼ tsp. salt
- ¼ tsp. ground black pepper
- 1 cup. drained kalamata olives
- 1 cup (4 oz.) Feta cheese, crumbled

Toss together tomato, cucumber, onion, oil and vinegar in a medium salad bowl. Sprinkle with parsley, salt and pepper. Toss again. Transfer to bowls and top with olives and Feta.

PER SERVING: Cal. 238, Fat 19g (Sat. 6g), Chol. 25mg, Fiber 2g, Pro. 6g, Carb. 13g, Sod. 671mg

Parsley Salad

PREP: 25 min. SERVES: 8 COST PER SERVING: ¢

- ¼ cup olive oil
- 1 Tbsp. red wine vinegar
- 1 shallot, minced
- 1 clove garlic, minced
- 1 tsp. Dijon mustard
- ¼ tsp. salt
- ⅛ tsp. ground black pepper

- Leaves from 2 bunches flat-leaf parsley (about 5 cups)
- Leaves from 2 bunches curly parsley (about 5 cups)
- ⅓ cup snipped fresh chives

1 Shake oil, vinegar, shallot, garlic, mustard, salt and pepper in a jar with a tight lid until combined. Set aside at room temperature.

2 Wash parsley leaves and spin dry. (Salad may be prepared to this point up to 6 hours ahead. Wrap parsley in damp paper towels and refrigerate in resealable plastic bags.)

3 To serve, toss parsley and chives with dressing in large bowl until well coated.

PER SERVING: Cal. 91, Fat 8g (Sat. 0g), Chol. 0mg, Fiber 3g, Pro. 2g, Carb. 5g, Sod. 117mg

HOW TO CHOOSE AND USE TOMATOES

There are hundreds of varieties of tomatoes. They are at their peak in the mid- to late summer, so you can enjoy the widest selection then. Ripe tomatoes are brightly colored and very fragrant at the stem end (where the leaves are). They should be firm, but not so hard that they don't give slightly when pressed gently with a fingertip.

Beefsteak tomatoes are large and bright red. They are delicious raw or cooked, and are particularly good when sliced on sandwiches or salads.

Cherry tomatoes are often served in salads and as garnishes. They are round, sweet and bite-size; their skin may be red or yellow.

Grape tomatoes are also called baby Romas. They are a hybrid and are small and sweet, similar to cherry tomatoes but slightly less juicy.

Heirloom tomatoes are found in a number of colors and textures and tend to have great flavor. Green Zebra, Brandywine and Hillbilly are just a few of the varieties available. Look for them at farmers' markets.

Roma tomatoes are also called Italian plum tomatoes. These egg-shaped tomatoes are best for cooked dishes.

Spinach and Avocado Salad

PREP: 10 min. SERVES: 8 COST PER SERVING: $

- 3 Tbsp. fresh lime juice
- 3 Tbsp. olive oil
- 1 Tbsp. chopped fresh cilantro
- 1 tsp. sugar
- ¼ tsp. ground cumin
- ¼ tsp. kosher salt
- ⅛ tsp. ground black pepper
- 1 ripe Haas avocado, peeled, pitted and thinly sliced
- 1 small red onion, thinly sliced
- 11 oz. baby spinach

Whisk lime juice, oil, cilantro, sugar, cumin, salt and pepper in a large serving bowl. Stir in avocado and red onion. Lay spinach on top. (Salad can be prepared and refrigerated up to 2 hours ahead.) Toss just before serving.

PER SERVING: Cal. 99, Fat 9g (Sat. 1g), Chol. 0mg, Fiber 2g, Pro. 2g, Carb. 5g, Sod. 93mg

Apple and Beet Salad

PREP: 15 min. COOK: 1 hr. and 15 min. CHILL: 2 hr. SERVES: 8 COST PER SERVING: $

- 8 beets
- 3 small red onions, unpeeled
- ¼ cup balsamic vinegar or red wine vinegar
- 2 Tbsp. vegetable oil
- 1½ tsp. kosher salt
- Ground black pepper
- 4 Granny Smith apples (1½ lb.)
- 1 Tbsp. fresh lemon juice
- ½ cup sour cream
- 12 curly red lettuce leaves, rinsed and dried
- ¼ cup crumbled blue cheese or goat cheese
- ¾ cup toasted pecan halves

1 Preheat oven to 400°F. Trim beet greens, leaving a 1-inch piece of stem. Scrub beets and dry on paper towels. Sort by size and tightly wrap and seal large and small beets separately, along with onions, in two heavy-duty aluminum-foil packages. Place packets on a baking sheet. Roast until beets are tender when pierced with a fork, about 1 hour for small beets and 1¼ hours for large. Unwrap packages and let cool for about 15 minutes. Peel and trim beets and onions, halve crosswise and thinly slice. Transfer to a bowl.

2 Add vinegar, oil, 1¼ tsp. salt and a pinch of pepper to beet mixture and stir until blended. Refrigerate, tightly covered, until chilled, at least 2 hours and up to 1 day. Taste and adjust seasonings before serving.

3 At least 2 hours and up to 12 hours before serving, peel, core and cut apples into ¼-inch wedges. Cut each slice crosswise into 3 pieces. Transfer to a bowl, add lemon juice and toss to coat. Add sour cream, remaining ¼ tsp. salt and a pinch of pepper and stir until blended. Cover and refrigerate apple mixture.

4 To serve, arrange lettuce leaves on a serving platter. Top with beet mixture and apple mixture separately. Sprinkle with cheese and pecans and serve.

PER SERVING: Cal. 256, Fat 16g (Sat. 4g), Chol. 13mg, Fiber 6g, Pro. 4g, Carb. 28g, Sod. 474mg

DON'T TOSS THE TOPS

A rich source of vitamin A, beet greens are delicious sautéed in a little olive oil. Be sure to wash them thoroughly and roughly chop them before cooking.

Horseradish–Cheddar Cheese Ball

PREP: 10 min. CHILL: 30 min. COOK: 10 min. SERVES: 8 COST PER SERVING: $

- 12 oz. extra-sharp Cheddar cheese, cut in 8 pieces
- 1 (8 oz.) package cream cheese
- 3 Tbsp. prepared hot horseradish
- ¼ tsp. cayenne pepper
- 1 cup pecan halves
- Crackers and bread sticks

1 Place Cheddar cheese in a food processor; process until finely chopped. Add cream cheese, horseradish and cayenne pepper; process until smooth.

2 Line a small bowl with two long sheets of plastic wrap. Spoon mixture into center, gather ends and twist together to form a ball. Chill for 30 minutes.

3 Preheat oven to 375°F. Spread pecans on a shallow baking sheet and roast for 8 to 10 minutes. Let cool; coarsely chop.

4 Unwrap cheese ball and pat pecan halves onto it. Serve with crackers and bread sticks.

PER SERVING: Cal. 378, Fat 36g (Sat. 17g), Chol. 75mg, Fiber 1g, Pro. 13g, Carb. 4g, Sod. 422mg

Guacamole

PREP: 10 minutes   SERVES: 8   COST PER SERVING: $$

- 3 ripe Haas avocados, peeled and pitted
- ½ cup fresh lime juice
- 2 Tbsp. fresh lemon juice
- 2 diced plum tomatoes
- 1 small yellow onion, finely chopped
- 2 cloves garlic, minced
- Minced fresh jalapeño to taste
- Salt to taste
- Tortilla chips

Mash avocados in a bowl. Stir in lime juice and lemon juice. Mix in tomatoes, onion, garlic and jalapeño. Season with salt. Lay plastic wrap directly on surface of guacamole and chill until ready to serve, up to 4 hours. Serve with tortilla chips.

PER SERVING: Cal. 126, Fat 11g (Sat. 2g), Chol. 0mg, Fiber 4g, Pro. 2g, Carb. 7g, Sod. 153mg

Quick Crab Cocktail

PREP: 5 min. SERVES: 12 COST PER SERVING: $$

- 16 oz. Neufchâtel cheese
- ⅔ cup ketchup
- 5 Tbsp. prepared horseradish sauce
- 1 lb. back-fin crabmeat

Place cheese in a shallow dish and spread with a spoon to coat bottom. Stir together ketchup and horseradish and spoon on top of cheese. Flake crab and scatter on top of sauce. Cover entire dish with plastic wrap and chill until ready to serve. Serve with crackers or bread.

PER SERVING: Cal. 156, Fat 11g (Sat. 6g), Chol. 67mg, Fiber 0g, Pro. 13g, Carb. 6g, Sod. 514mg

Creamy Ginger-Parsnip Soup

PREP: 15 min.   COOK: 25 min.   YIELD: about 2 qt.   COST PER SERVING: ¢

- 2 lb. parsnips, peeled and cut into 1-inch pieces
- 1 sweet potato, peeled and and cut into 1-inch pieces
- 1 onion, chopped
- 1 (2-inch) piece peeled fresh ginger
- 1 quart chicken broth
- 1 cup heavy cream
- 2 cups water
- ½ tsp. kosher salt
- Black pepper to taste
- 1 cup chopped toasted walnuts
- ¼ cup minced chives

1 Combine parsnips, sweet potato, onion, ginger and chicken broth in medium saucepan. Heat over medium-high heat until broth comes to a boil. Reduce heat and simmer for 25 minutes.

2 Transfer half of the mixture to a blender and add heavy cream. Puree until smooth and transfer to a bowl. Transfer remaining mixture to the blender and add 1 cup water.

3 Return pureed mixtures to saucepan; stir in remaining 1 cup water and ½ tsp. kosher salt. Season with black pepper and heat over medium heat until warmed through. To serve, sprinkle with chopped toasted walnuts and minced chives.

PER SERVING (1 CUP): Cal. 332, Fat 22g (Sat. 8g), Chol. 41mg, Fiber 7g, Pro. 5g, Carb. 31g, Sod. 805mg

KNOW YOUR PARSNIPS

Parsnips look like white carrots and have a sweet flavor similar to carrots or turnips.

Buy in the winter. Frost converts the starch in parsnips to sugar, so the vegetable is sweetest during cold months.

Select well. Look for small-to-medium-size roots that are firm and have uniform ivory skin and no spots.

Store in the refrigerator. Wrap unwashed parsnips in paper towels or a plastic bag and refrigerate for up to two weeks.

Prepare like a carrot. Scrub well, trim off ends and peel skin with a vegetable peeler as you would a carrot or turnip. Then bake, boil or steam.

Roasted Red Pepper Soup

PREP: 15 min.   COOK: 30 min.   SERVES: 8   COST PER SERVING: **$$$**

- 1 stick (½ cup) unsalted butter
- 6 onions, finely chopped
- 4 cloves garlic, minced
- 4 (14 oz.) cans Italian plum tomatoes with their juice
- 4 (13.75 oz.) cans chicken or vegetable broth
- 1 (15 oz.) can crushed tomatoes
- 4 (7 oz.) jars roasted red peppers, chopped
- 2 Tbsp. Pernod or other anise-flavored liqueur, optional
- 1 Tbsp. fresh thyme leaves, plus more for garnish
- ½ tsp. kosher salt
- ½ tsp. black pepper
- 1 cup sour cream
- 2 tsp. grated lemon peel

1 Melt butter in a Dutch oven or other large, heavy pot over medium heat. Add onions and cook, stirring, until softened, about 10 minutes. Add garlic and cook, stirring, for 2 minutes. Add plum tomatoes and their juice, chicken broth and crushed tomatoes; bring to a boil; then simmer for 5 minutes. Add red peppers, Pernod (if using), thyme, salt and pepper; bring to a boil; then simmer for 5 minutes longer.

2 Stir together sour cream and lemon peel in a bowl. Cover and refrigerate.

DON'T WASTE THE LEFTOVERS!

Toss any leftover peppers on some good Italian bread, layer with ham, salami or cheese and sprinkle with a little olive oil.

3 Strain soup into a large bowl. Puree strained solids in batches in a blender or food processor, adding soup liquid to blend. Strain again over same bowl and discard solids. Wipe out Dutch oven, add soup and bring to a simmer.

4 Strain soup into a serving bowl, dollop sour cream on top and garnish with thyme.

PER SERVING (1 CUP): Cal. 313, Fat 20g (Sat. 11g), Chol. 51mg, Fiber 5g, Pro. 6g, Carb. 25g, Sod. 1,995mg

Broccoli-Cheese Soup

PREP: **10 min.** COOK: **15 min.** YIELD: **2 qt.** COST PER SERVING: **$**

- 4 Tbsp. unsalted butter
- 1 large onion, finely diced
- ¼ cup all-purpose flour
- 1 qt. chicken broth
- 6 cups frozen broccoli florets (about 1½ lb.), thawed
- 1½ cups milk
- 2 cups shredded sharp Cheddar cheese
- 2 cups prepared croutons, for serving

1 Melt butter over medium heat in a large saucepan. Add onion and cook, stirring occasionally, until softened, about 4 minutes. Add flour and cook, stirring to make a paste, for 2 minutes. Gradually whisk in broth and then bring to a boil. Add broccoli and cook, stirring often, until tender, about 3 minutes. Remove from heat.

2 Puree broccoli mixture in batches using a blender. Transfer batches to a large bowl. Return purée to saucepan, place over medium heat and bring to a simmer. Gradually whisk in milk and 1 cup cheese. Ladle soup into bowls. Top each serving with croutons and a sprinkling of remaining cheese.

PER SERVING (1 CUP): Cal. 272, Fat 17g (Sat. 11g), Chol. 52mg, Fiber 3g, Pro. 12g, Carb. 16g, Sod. 927mg

BLEND WITH CARE

You can use either a food processor or a blender to puree soup. Just be sure to work in small batches (don't fill the container more than halfway), or you'll have hot liquid spilling out of the top.

Shrimp-Avocado Tacos page 33

Penne with Sweet Peas and Prosciutto page 46

Grilled Steak with Roasted Potatoes page 42

Yogurt-Marinated Chicken Kabobs page 28

Asian Chicken and Rice Noodle Salad   page 51

Main Dishes

The most-asked question in the world may very well be "What's for dinner?" In this chapter we answer it in 32 delicious ways. From no-cook options such as **Chicken-Mango Wraps** (page 29) to healthy twists on kids' favorites like **Chicken Nuggets with Sweet Fries** (page 27) to sumptuous slow-cooker creations such as **Pork Carnitas** (page 36), you've got a tasty choice for every night of the week.

INTENSIFY THE FLAVORS!

Make more of a meal by cooking with these flavor enhancers.

Give it gusto with garlic. Mince garlic and toss it in salad dressings, sauté it in sauces, stir it into stir-fries and mix it into marinades. Crushed garlic adds zip to soups or roasting meats.

Jazz it up with anchovies. Top a homemade pizza with canned anchovies or use them to flavor pasta sauces or salad dressings. The flavor can be strong, so use them sparingly. Unopened cans of anchovies will keep for up to a year. Once opened, they will keep, wrapped in plastic and refrigerated, for up to two days.

Add a punch with chorizo. Thinly slice this spicy pork sausage (which is flavored with garlic, chili powder and other seasonings) and add it to enchiladas, casseroles, soups and stews. Chorizo also tastes great paired with seafood, potatoes and beans.

Chicken Stew with Green Olives   page 25

Extra-Juicy Pork Chop   page 37

Sautéed Chicken with Fresh Blueberry Sauce

PREP: **10** min.   COOK: **15** min.   SERVES: **2**   COST PER SERVING: **$$$**

- 4 large skinless, boneless chicken breast halves (7 oz. to 8 oz. each)
- Salt and ground black pepper to taste
- 4 Tbsp. all-purpose flour
- 2 Tbsp. olive oil
- 2 shallots, chopped
- ⅔ cup dry white wine
- 2 cups reduced-sodium chicken broth
- 1⅓ cups fresh blueberries
- Pinch sugar
- 2 Tbsp. unsalted butter

1 Season chicken breast halves with salt and pepper. Coat with flour; shake off excess.

2 Heat olive oil in a large skillet over medium-high heat. Brown chicken, turning once, about 10 minutes. Transfer chicken to a plate and cover with foil.

3 Add shallots to skillet and cook on medium heat, stirring, for 1 minute. Pour in white wine and boil for 2 minutes. Add chicken broth and bring to a boil. Add blueberries and sugar and simmer until liquid is reduced by half, about 3 minutes. Remove from heat and stir in butter; season with salt and pepper.

4 To serve, slice chicken crosswise into ½-inch slices and arrange each breast on a plate. Spoon sauce over and serve.

PER SERVING: Cal. 461, Fat 18g (5g Sat.), Chol. 133mg, Fiber 2g, Pro. 49g, Carb. 19g, Sod. 173mg

KNOW YOUR BLUEBERRIES

Blueberries are full of antioxidants, which protect against cancer and heart disease. So eat plenty of them!

Cultivated blueberries are those that you often see in the supermarket produce section. They are usually a hybrid of highbush and lowbush varieties and are sweet, plump and fleshy.

Wild, or lowbush, blueberries are smaller than cultivated ones and have a more complex flavor, which is sweet yet tart and somewhat spicy. They grow in colder climes, and you'll find them only in farmers' markets because they don't ship well.

Crispy Baked Chicken

PREP: 10 min. BAKE: 45 min. SERVES: 4 COST PER SERVING: **$$**

- 1 cup cream of mushroom soup
- ½ cup milk
- 1 Tbsp. prepared pesto
- 2 cups plain dried bread crumbs
- 1 tsp. dried oregano
- ¼ tsp. kosher salt
- ¼ tsp. pepper
- 1 (4 lb.) chicken, cut in eighths (backbone reserved for another use)

1 Arrange rack in upper third of oven. Preheat oven to 425°F.

2 In a large bowl, whisk together soup, milk and pesto. Combine bread crumbs, oregano, salt and pepper in another bowl. Dip chicken pieces in soup mixture, then roll in crumbs, coating well. Place chicken skin side up on a large baking sheet.

3 Roast chicken in the upper third of oven until golden and crisp on top and cooked through, about 45 minutes.

PER SERVING: Cal. 1,156, Fat 71g (Sat. 19g), Chol. 349mg, Fiber 3g, Pro. 78g, Carb. 45g, Sod. 1,290 mg

CUT THE FAT

For a lower-fat version, use skinless chicken pieces instead.

Super-Easy Apricot Chicken

PREP: **15 min.** COOK: **4 hr. and 10 min.** SERVES: **4** COST PER SERVING: **$**

- 12 dried apricots
- 8 medium chicken thighs (about 2½ lb.)
- Salt and pepper
- 2 Tbsp. unsalted butter
- 2 Tbsp. vegetable oil
- 1 onion, sliced
- 1 cup chicken broth

1 Rinse apricots and scatter them in a slow cooker. Pat chicken dry; season with salt and pepper. Melt butter in oil in a large skillet over medium-high heat. Cook thighs until golden brown, 3 to 5 minutes per side. (Brown in batches to avoid crowding skillet.) Arrange over apricots.

2 Pour off all but 1 Tbsp. fat in skillet. Add onion and cook until just soft, 2 to 4 minutes.

3 Add broth to skillet; turn heat to high. Bring to a boil, loosening browned bits.

4 Pour contents of skillet over apricots and chicken. Cover and cook on low heat for 4 hours.

5 Carefully transfer thighs to a serving dish (they tend to fall apart easily); cover with foil to keep warm. Pour remaining contents into a saucepan. Boil, stirring often, until reduced and thickened, about 10 minutes. Pour over chicken.

PER SERVING: Cal. 379, Fat 23g (Sat. 7g), Chol. 119mg, Fiber 1g, Pro. 32g, Carb. 9g, Sod. 436mg

Chicken Cacciatore

PREP: **10 min.** COOK: **4 hr.** SERVES: **4** COST PER SERVING: **$$$**

- 1 Tbsp. olive oil
- 3 cloves garlic, smashed
- 1 (14 oz.) Spanish onion
- 1 green bell pepper, sliced into ½-inch-wide strips
- 1 yellow bell pepper, sliced into ½-inch-wide strips
- 1 (8 oz.) package baby bella mushrooms, quartered
- 1 (4 lb.) broiler chicken, quartered
- 1 tsp. kosher salt
- Ground black pepper
- 1 (28 oz.) can crushed tomatoes
- ½ lb. uncooked rotini
- ¼ cup finely chopped fresh parsley
- Freshly grated Parmesan cheese, for serving

1 Heat oil in a small skillet over medium heat. Add garlic and cook, stirring, until golden, about 2 minutes; transfer to slow cooker.

2 Add onion, bell peppers and mushrooms. Put chicken on top; sprinkle with salt and pepper. Pour in crushed tomatoes; cover and cook for 4 hours on high or 8 hours on low. Chicken should be very tender.

3 Bring a pot of salted water to a boil and cook rotini according to package directions until al dente. Drain and transfer to a large serving bowl.

4 Transfer chicken to 4 plates. Skim fat from surface of sauce and discard. Stir parsley into sauce. Spoon some sauce over chicken. Serve remaining sauce with pasta and cheese.

PER SERVING: Cal. 1,159, Fat 63g (Sat. 17g), Chol. 324mg, Fiber 7g, Pro. 83g, Carb. 61g, Sod. 1,231mg

THE BEST CHEESE

For the best flavor, use imported Italian Parmigiano-Reggiano cheese to complete this warm and tasty meal.

Chicken and Summer Vegetable Stew

PREP: 15 min.   COOK: 25 min.   SERVES: 6   COST PER SERVING: **$$**

- 2 chicken breast halves on the bone
- 1 tsp. salt
- ½ tsp. pepper
- 1 Tbsp all-purpose flour
- 2 Tbsp olive oil
- 3 Tbsp butter
- 1 yellow squash, thinly sliced
- 1 small zucchini, thinly sliced
- 1 (10 oz.) box frozen baby lima beans, thawed
- 2½ cups yellow corn (from about 3 medium ears)
- 3 ripe plum tomatoes, seeded and cut into ⅓-inch dice
- 4 cups chicken broth
- ¼ cup snipped fresh chives (½-inch lengths)

1 Season chicken breasts with ½ tsp. each salt and pepper, then sprinkle with flour. Heat olive oil in a heavy 2½-quart pot over medium heat. Add chicken, skin side down, and cook, covered, until nicely golden, about 7 minutes. Turn chicken breasts over, cover and cook until juices run clear when chicken is pierced with a knife, about 8 minutes. Remove chicken from heat, transfer to a board and let cool. Set pot aside.

2 Melt butter over medium heat in the same pot. Add squash, zucchini, lima beans and corn and cook, stirring often, until squash is wilted, 4 to 5 minutes.

3 While vegetables are cooking, cut chicken into ½-inch chunks. Add to vegetables along with tomatoes and broth. Season with remaining ½ tsp. salt and ½ teaspoon pepper and cook, stirring until heated through, about 3 minutes. Sprinkle chives on top just before serving.

PER SERVING: Cal. 381, Fat 22g (Sat. 7g), Chol. 76mg, Fiber 4g, Pro. 26g, Carb. 21g, Sod. 1,333 mg

Chicken Stew with Green Olives

PREP: **10 min.** COOK: **4 hr.** SERVES: **4** COST PER SERVING: **$$$$**

- 1 (28 oz.) can whole tomatoes, drained and coarsely chopped
- 1½ cups chicken broth
- 1 onion, sliced
- 1 clove garlic, minced
- 1 tsp. ground cumin
- 1 tsp. paprika
- ½ tsp. turmeric
- 1½ Tbsp. olive oil
- 1 (3 lb.) quartered chicken, skinned
- 2 tsp. kosher salt
- ½ tsp. black pepper
- ½ cup pitted green olives
- Grated peel of 1 lemon
- Cooked couscous
- ¼ cup sliced almonds, toasted

ALL ABOUT OLIVES

Green olives are picked before they ripen, and are usually brined. Look for quality olives in plastic bins in your market's deli section.

1 Place tomatoes, 1 cup broth, onion, garlic, cumin, paprika and turmeric into slow cooker.

2 Heat 1 Tbsp. oil in a large skillet over medium-high heat. Season chicken with salt and pepper, place in skillet and cook, turning, until browned, about 8 minutes. Transfer to slow cooker. Pour remaining ½ cup broth into skillet, scraping brown bits from bottom of pan. Pour liquid into slow cooker.

3 Cook chicken on high for 4 hours. Thirty minutes before chicken is finished, stir in olives and lemon peel.

4 Remove chicken from slow cooker; let cool. Remove meat from bones, then return meat to slow cooker.

5 Serve stew on top of cooked couscous and sprinkle with almonds.

PER SERVING: Cal. 382, Fat 17g (Sat. 2g), Chol. 115mg, Fiber 5g, Pro. 40g, Carb. 14g, Sod. 2,135mg

Potato, Corn and Chicken Chowder

PREP: **15 min.** COOK: **3 hr. 10 min.** SERVES: **6** COST PER SERVING: **$$**

- 1 large sweet onion (such as Vidalia), chopped
- 6 medium Yukon Gold potatoes (about 2½ lb.), peeled and quartered
- 1 (14.5 oz.) can low-sodium chicken broth
- 1½ cups water
- 2 cups cooked or frozen corn
- 2 cups shredded or diced cooked chicken
- 2 ripe plum tomatoes, finely diced
- ⅔ cup heavy cream
- Ground black pepper to taste
- 3 Tbsp. olive oil
- ½ Tbsp. finely chopped fresh basil
- ¼ tsp. kosher salt

1 Put chopped onion slow cooker and top with potatoes. Add broth and 1½ cups water. Cover and cook for 3 hours on high.

2 Coarsely mash potatoes; stir in corn, chicken, tomatoes and cream. Cover and let cook until heated through, about 10 minutes. (To make chowder ahead, prepare to this point, let cool, cover and chill for up to 3 days.) Season with pepper to taste.

3 Just before serving, stir together oil, basil and salt. Drizzle basil oil over each serving.

PER SERVING: Cal. 455, Fat 22g (Sat. 8g), Chol. 79mg, Fiber 5g, Pro. 20g, Carb. 47g, Sod. 159mg

CHOWDER IDEAS

Choose the right potato. Yukon Golds work best in this recipe because they're not overly starchy.

Serve up a side dish. Bacon-Cheddar Muffins or Corn Bread (page 69) go perfectly with this chowder.

Use leftovers. Pick up a large rotisserie chicken and reserve 2 cups of meat for this recipe. Serve the rest the next day with oven-baked fries and cole slaw.

Chicken Nuggets and Sweet Fries

PREP: **15 min.**   COOK: **35 min.**   SERVES: **4**   COST PER SERVING: **$**

- 1½ lb. sweet potatoes, peeled and cut into ½-inch sticks
- 1 Tbsp. olive oil
- Salt and ground black pepper
- ½ tsp. cumin
- 1¼ cups panko bread crumbs
- 3 chicken breast halves (1½ lb.), cut into 1½-inch chunks
- ⅔ cup honey mustard

1 Preheat oven to 400°F. Toss sweet potatoes in a large bowl with oil, salt and cumin. Spread on an oiled baking sheet.

2 Place panko in a shallow pan or pie plate. Toss chicken chunks with salt and pepper in a large bowl. Stir in honey mustard and toss to coat thoroughly. Place chicken chunks, several at a time, into panko and press on all sides to adhere. Spread on an oiled baking sheet.

3 Bake sweet potatoes and chicken about 20 minutes, turning occasionally with a metal spatula. Increase heat to 450°F. Remove chicken after 5 minutes, once it's golden and cooked through; tent with foil to keep warm until ready to serve. Cook sweet potatoes until golden brown and crisp, 10 to 15 minutes longer.

PER SERVING: Cal. 532, Fat 7g (Sat. 1g), Chol. 99mg, Fiber 2g, Pro. 44g, Carb. 67g, Sod. 376mg

NUGGETS OF WISDOM

If you're really pressed for time at the end of the day, try these shortcuts:

Buy cooked chicken breasts from a deli counter. Cut them into 1-inch chunks and toss with honey mustard and coat with chopped almonds, pecans or walnuts. Bake in a 375°F oven until the nuts are golden and fragrant, about 8 minutes.

Buy frozen sweet-potato fries and cook according to the package directions.

Yogurt-Marinated Chicken Kebabs

PREP: **10 min.** MARINATE: **2 hr.** COOK: **15 min.** SERVES: **4** COST PER SERVING: **$$**

- 8 (9-inch) wooden skewers
- 1⅓ cups low-fat plain yogurt
- 2 Tbsp. plus 1 tsp. fresh lemon juice
- 1⅓ tsp. ground coriander
- 3 large cloves garlic, crushed
- Salt and ground black pepper
- 2 lb. skinless, boneless chicken breasts, cut into 1-inch cubes
- 1 large red bell pepper, cored, seeded and cut into 1-inch chunks
- 1 small onion, cut into 1-inch chunks
- 1 Tbsp. olive oil

NOT JUST CHICKEN

These kebabs are just as delicious made with with beef cubes or shrimp.

1 Soak skewers in water for 30 minutes prior to grilling. Combine yogurt, lemon juice, coriander and garlic in a large resealable plastic bag; season with pepper. Add chicken and seal bag, kneading bag to coat completely. Refrigerate for at least 2 hours or overnight.

2 Wipe marinade off chicken; discard marinade. Thread onto skewers, alternating with pepper and onion pieces. Season with salt.

3 Heat grill pan over medium-high heat, brush with oil, add kebabs (in batches if necessary) and cover with foil. Grill on medium heat, turning on all sides, until chicken is cooked through, about 12 minutes. Serve kebabs with grilled pita bread, rice and a green vegetable or salad.

PER SERVING: Cal. 357, Fat 7g (Sat. 2g), Chol. 137mg, Fiber 2g, Pro. 57g, Carb. 14g, Sod. 199mg

Chicken-Mango Wraps

PREP: **20 min.**   SERVES: **4**   COST PER SERVING: **$$**

- ¼ cup mayonnaise
- 1 Tbsp. apricot or peach jam
- 1 tsp. minced jalapeño
- 4 (8-inch) spinach wraps, warmed
- 3 cups baby spinach leaves
- 4 cups thickly sliced cooked chicken (about 12 oz.)
- 1 ripe mango, pitted, peeled and sliced ½ inch thick
- 1 ripe avocado, pitted, peeled and sliced ½ inch thick
- 1½ cups alfalfa sprouts

1 Stir mayonnaise, jam and jalapeño together in a small bowl.

2 Lay wraps flat on a work area and spread them with mayonnaise mixture. Layer spinach leaves flat down the center of wraps. Top with chicken, mango, avocado and sprouts.

3 Roll wraps snugly, cut in half and serve.

PER SERVING: Cal. 532, Fat 25g (Sat. 4g), Chol. 77mg, Fiber 6g, Pro. 33g, Carb. 43g, Sod. 402mg

CHANGE IT UP

For variety, use a different flavor wrap. Sun-dried tomato, honey-wheat and jalapeño are just a few of the flavors available.

Oven-Fried Fish and Chips

PREP: 15 min. BAKE: 30 min. SERVES: 4 COST PER SERVING: **$**

The chips:

- 2 large baking potatoes, scrubbed
- 1 Tbsp. olive oil
- ¼ tsp. dried thyme
- ½ tsp. kosher salt
- ¼ tsp. ground black pepper

The fish:

- 4 (6 oz.) grouper, halibut or cod fillets (about ¾ inch thick)
- ⅓ cup milk
- ½ cup cornmeal
- ¼ tsp. hot chili powder
- ½ tsp. kosher salt
- ¼ tsp. ground black pepper
- 2 Tbsp. olive oil
- Lemon wedges, for serving
- Malt vinegar, for serving

1 Arrange oven racks in top and bottom thirds of oven and preheat oven to 450°F.

2 Slice potatoes crosswise into ¼-inch thick rounds, transfer to a bowl and toss with 1 Tbsp. olive oil. Arrange on a large, foil-lined baking sheet. Sprinkle with thyme, ½ tsp. salt and ¼ tsp. pepper. Bake in bottom of oven for 30 minutes.

3 Meanwhile, combine fish and milk in a large bowl; turn fish to coat. Toss together cornmeal, chili powder, ½ tsp. salt and ¼ tsp. pepper in a shallow bowl. Add 1 fish fillet and coat with cornmeal mixture. Transfer fillet to a large plate and repeat with remaining fillets.

4 Heat a large cast-iron skillet over medium heat. Add 2 Tbsp. oil, swirling to coat pan. Add fillets and cook until nicely crusted on bottom, about 2 minutes; carefully turn and then transfer skillet to top rack in oven. Cook until golden and firm when pressed in center, about 6 minutes. Serve with fresh lemon and vinegar.

PER SERVING: Cal. 472, Fat 16g (Sat. 2g), Chol. 58mg, Fiber 5g, Pro. 42g, Carb. 38g, Sod. 938mg

Grilled Fish with Fruit Salsa

PREP: **10 min.** BROIL: **6 min.** SERVES: **4** COST PER SERVING: **$$**

- 1 large peach or 1 small mango
- 1 cup medium prepared salsa
- ¼ cup olive oil
- 1 Tbsp. fresh lime juice
- 1 Tbsp. honey
- Pinch of salt
- 6 cups (4 oz.) lightly packed tender salad greens
- 4 (6 oz.) tilapia fillets or other mild white fish

1 Peel and pit peach and cut into ½-inch cubes. Transfer to a medium bowl and stir prepared salsa and peach together.

2 Combine 2 Tbsp. oil, lime juice, honey and salt in a large salad bowl and whisk together. Add tender salad greens, but do not toss.

3 Preheat broiler and line a baking sheet with foil. Brush remaining 2 Tbsp. oil on both sides of fillets. Arrange fish on foil-lined baking sheet and broil until fish is just cooked through, about 6 minutes. Transfer fish to serving plates and top with salsa. Toss salad and place on plates next to fish.

PER SERVING: Cal. 323, Fat 18g (Sat. 2g), Chol. 82mg, Fiber 2g, Pro. 36g, Carb. 12g, Sod. 434mg

---

GRILLED FISH FACTS

Freshen up homemade salsa. Add diced fruit to your own tomato salsa. And don't use it just on fish—it goes well with chicken, too.

Cook tilapia just right. Tilapia is a firm, mild white fish that cooks quickly.

Use other fish varieties. Thin gray sole or red snapper fillets would be fine substitutes for this dish.

Try mâche lettuce. It's also called lamb's lettuce or corn salad. Buy it just 1 or 2 days before you need it, because it's perishable. Serve this dish with roasted baby potatoes or rice.

Jamaican Red Snapper with Pan-Fried Bananas

PREP: 15 min. COOK: 17 min. SERVES: 4 COST PER SERVING: **$$$$**

- 1 cup plain dried bread crumbs
- 2 tsp. five-spice powder
- 1 tsp. dried thyme, crumbled
- 1 tsp. ground allspice
- 1 tsp. kosher salt
- ⅛ to ½ tsp. cayenne pepper
- 2 large eggs
- 1½ lb. small red snapper or grey sole fillets
- 6 Tbsp. vegetable oil, for frying
- 4 firm bananas, sliced ½ inch thick
- Lime wedges, for serving

1 Toss together bread crumbs, five-spice powder, thyme, allspice, salt and cayenne in a shallow bowl. Beat eggs with a fork in a second shallow bowl. Turn fish fillets one at a time in crumbs, then dip them in beaten eggs to coat and then coat again with crumb mixture; place on a plate.

2 Heat 2 Tbsp. oil in a large skillet over medium heat until hot. Add half of fish and cook until golden and crisp on bottom, 2 to 3 minutes; turn and cook until crisp on other side, 2 to 3 minutes more. Transfer fish to a plate and keep in a warm oven while you repeat with remaining fish and 2 Tbsp. more oil.

3 Heat remaining 2 Tbsp. oil in a large nonstick skillet over medium-high heat. Pan-fry bananas until golden on both sides, about 4 minutes. Serve bananas and lime wedges with fish.

PER SERVING: Cal. 614, Fat 28g (Sat. 5g), Chol. 170mg, Fiber 4g, Pro. 43g, Carb. 49g, Sod. 824mg

KNOW YOUR BANANAS

Bananas fall into two categories: the eating banana and the cooking banana, or plantain. There are roughly 150 species, but here are the varieties you're most likely to see in the produce section of the supermarket.

Cavendish banana: This is the banana you know best. It has a thick skin that withstands bruising, and it's available year-round.

Dwarf banana: Smaller than the Cavendish, it has a thinner skin and sweeter taste as well. One type, the Lady Finger, is four to five inches long and has thin, light yellow skin and very sweet flesh.

Plantain: This large firm variety is green, brown or reddish in color. It is the ideal banana for frying or baking like a potato.

Red banana: This short, chunky banana has a purplish red peel. It's firm-fleshed and sweet.

Shrimp-Avocado Tacos

PREP: 15 min. **COOK:** 5 min. **SERVES:** 4 **COST PER SERVING:** **$$$$**

- 1 dozen fresh 6- or 7-inch corn tortillas
- 2 ripe Hass avocados
- 1 lime, quartered
- 1 to 2 medium tomatoes, finely diced
- ½ tsp. salt
- 1 small onion
- 1 small head green leaf lettuce
- ½ Tbsp. corn or vegetable oil
- 1 lb. easy-peel medium shrimp, peeled and halved lengthwise
- 1 tsp. Mexican-style hot chili powder
- ½ tsp. ground cumin

1 Preheat oven to 325°F. Wrap tortillas in foil and place in oven.

2 Halve and pit avocados. Score flesh with a knife to make small, diced pieces and then scoop pieces into a bowl. Squeeze in juice from lime quarters, add diced tomatoes and salt. Toss mixture gently and set aside.

3 Finely chop onion and put pieces in a small bowl. Slice lettuce into small, thin ribbons and put in a separate bowl.

4 Heat oil in a heavy skillet over medium-high heat until hot but not smoking. Add prepared shrimp and sprinkle chili powder and cumin on top; cook, stirring, until shrimp is pink and curls up, 2 to 3 minutes. Transfer cooked shrimp to a bowl. Remove tortillas from oven.

5 Serve warm tortillas with shrimp, lettuce, onion and avocado-tomato mixture.

PER SERVING: Cal. 493, Fat 21g (Sat. 3g), Chol. 172mg, Fiber 11g, Pro. 31g, Carb. 51g, Sod. 490mg

Shrimp and Vegetable Stir-Fry

PREP: **15 min.** COOK: **10 min.** SERVES: **4** COST PER SERVING: **$$**

- ¾ cup chicken broth
- ¼ cup fresh orange juice
- 2 Tbsp. soy sauce
- 1 Tbsp. cornstarch
- ½ tsp. sugar
- 2 Tbsp. peanut oil or vegetable oil
- 1 lb. frozen deveined large shrimp, thawed and peeled
- 3 cloves garlic, minced
- 1 (1 lb.) bag frozen stir-fry vegetables, thawed and drained
- 4 cups steamed brown rice, for serving (cook about 2 cups dry)

1 Whisk together broth, orange juice, soy sauce, cornstarch and sugar in a small bowl; set aside.

2 Heat oil in wok or large nonstick skillet over medium-high heat. Add shrimp and stir-fry for 2 minutes. Add half of garlic and stir-fry about 2 more minutes. Transfer to a plate.

3 Add vegetables and cook, stirring, until heated through, about 3 minutes. Stir sauce again and add to pan, stirring until thickened, about 2 minutes. Return shrimp to pan and toss to coat. Serve with rice.

PER SERVING: Cal. 472, Fat 11g (Sat. 2g), Chol. 172mg, Fiber 5g, Pro. 32g, Carb. 59g, Sod. 880mg

---

STIR-FRY SUGGESTIONS

Stock up on frozen vegetables. You can whip up this dish anytime by having a variety of frozen stir-fry vegetables on hand. Just thaw veggies in the microwave before cooking.

Choose solidly frozen shrimp. Look at and feel the bag in the freezer case. Make sure the packaging is airtight and the shrimp are encased in ice and rock-hard.

Thaw in the refrigerator. Don't defrost frozen shrimp at room temperature. If the shrimp smells like ammonia after you've thawed it, it has gone bad: Throw it out immediately.

Pork Carnitas

PREP: 10 min. COOK: 6 hr. and 10 min. SERVES: 6 COST PER SERVING: $

- 1 onion, sliced
- 2 Tbsp. chopped chipotles in adobo or 2 fresh jalapeño chiles, seeded and sliced
- 2 to 3 lb. boned pork butt or shoulder
- 4 cloves garlic, slivered
- Salt and ground black pepper
- 1 Tbsp. vegetable oil
- 1 (14 oz.) package 6-inch corn tortillas

1 Place onion, chipotles and ¼ cup water in slow cooker. Stir to combine. Make incisions all over pork with a knife and insert garlic. Season roast with salt and pepper.

2 Heat a large pan over medium-high heat and add oil. Put roast in pan and brown on all sides, about 8 minutes. Transfer roast to slow cooker. Pour ½ cup water into pan and stir over low heat, using a wooden spoon to scrape up browned bits. Pour liquid into slow cooker. Cover and cook on high for 6 hours.

3 Remove roast from slow cooker and let cool. Shred pork, using two forks to pull meat apart. Return pulled pork to slow cooker and stir to combine with onions, chipotles and juices.

4 Serve pork with warm tortillas and toppings of your choice.

PER SERVING: Cal. 471, Fat 19g (Sat. 6g), Chol. 129mg, Fiber 4g, Pro. 41g, Carb. 33g, Sod. 161mg

ALL ABOUT TORTILLAS

Tortillas are round, flat, unleavened breads that resemble very thin pancakes. They can be made from corn or wheat flour.

Keep tortillas refrigerated, not frozen. They should last for up to 3 weeks, kept in a sealed bag. Frozen tortillas lose flavor and moisture.

Add some color to your plate. Use tortillas made with blue or red corn, which can be found at Mexican grocery stores. The flavor is the same, but the color contrast can be beautiful!

Extra-Juicy Pork Chops

PREP: **5 min.**   COOK: **20 min.**   SERVES: **4**   COST PER SERVING: **$**

- 4 (1-inch-thick) pork chops (10 oz. each)
- Kosher salt
- Ground black pepper
- 1 Tbsp. olive oil
- 1 red onion, halved and sliced ¼-inch thick
- 1 cup dry white wine or water
- 2 tsp. fresh thyme leaves
- ½ tsp. sugar
- 1 Tbsp. butter

1 Season both sides of pork chops with salt and pepper. Heat a large skillet over medium-high heat. Add olive oil. Add pork chops, reduce heat to medium and cook, turning once, until nicely browned and juices run clear, about 10 minutes. Transfer to a plate and tent with foil to keep warm.

2 Pour off extra grease from pan. Put onion in same pan and cook for 3 minutes. Stir in wine and thyme. Increase heat to medium-high and bring liquid to a boil. Reduce heat and simmer until liquid is reduced by half, about 3 minutes. Stir in sugar. Add butter and any accumulated juices from pork and stir to combine.

3 Serve pork chops with onion slices and pan juices spooned on top.

PER SERVING: Cal. 416, Fat 25g (Sat. 9g), Chol. 110mg, Fiber 1g, Pro. 37g, Carb. 5g, Sod. 104mg

EXPERIMENT WITH FLAVOR

Thicken the sauce with other ingredients, such as prepared mustard and cream, stirring them in at the end. Also, try other fresh herbs that go well with pork, such as tarragon or rosemary.

Pork Tenderloin with Sautéed Apples

PREP: **9 min.** COOK: **21 min.** SERVES: **4** COST PER SERVING: **$$**

- 1 pork tenderloin (about 1 lb.)
- ¾ tsp. salt
- ½ tsp. ground black pepper
- ¼ cup all-purpose flour
- 2 Tbsp. olive oil
- ¼ cup minced onion
- ⅓ cup white wine or apple cider
- 1 cup chicken broth
- 1 small golden delicious apple, quartered, cored and thinly sliced
- 2 Tbsp. unsalted butter

1 Cut pork into 12 pieces and pound into scaloppine about ⅓-inch thick. Season with ½ tsp. each salt and pepper, then dust with flour.

2 Heat 1 Tbsp. oil in a large, nonstick skillet over medium-high heat. Add half of the pork, without crowding pan, and cook, until nicely browned on bottom, about 3 minutes; turn and cook until pork is cooked through, about 3 minutes more. Transfer pork to a plate. Repeat with remaining oil and pork.

3 Add onion and wine to pan; cook over medium heat, stirring, until pan is nearly dry, about 2 minutes. Add broth and apple; simmer until liquid is reduced by half, about 5 minutes. Add butter and remaining ½ tsp. salt; stir until incorporated. Remove pan from heat, add pork slices to sauce and turn to coat.

4 Arrange pork on plates, spoon sauce and apples on top and serve.

PER SERVING: Cal. 315, Fat 18g (Sat. 6g), Chol. 89mg, Fiber 1g, Pro. 25g, Carb. 11g, Sod. 820mg

HOW TO CHOOSE & USE PORK

Choose fresh meat. Look for pork that is firm to the touch and has a pink color with a grayish tint. If the fat is yellowish, the meat is close to being spoiled.

Trim the fat. For leaner pork chops, trim fat to ⅛ of an inch. You want to leave a little fat to help keep meat moist during cooking.

Store pork safely. Sealed, prepackaged fresh pork can be kept in the refrigerator for 2 to 4 days or in the freezer for up to 6 months. Freeze it in heavy-duty foil or plastic bags. Cover sharp bones with extra foil or freezer wrap so they don't poke through.

Spicy Skirt Steak Chimichurri and Corn Chili

PREP: 10 min. COOK: 14 min. SERVES: 4 COST PER SERVING: $$

The chimichurri (makes 1½ cups):

- Leaves from 1 bunch cilantro leaves (about 2 cups packed)
- 2 cloves garlic
- ½ cup olive oil
- 1 Tbsp. fresh lemon juice
- 1 tsp. kosher salt

The steak:

- 1 (1½ lb.) skirt steak, cut into 4-inch portions
- ½ tsp. ground cumin
- ½ tsp. hot chili powder
- ½ tsp. kosher salt
- ½ tsp. ground black pepper

The corn chili:

- 2 Tbsp. unsalted butter
- 2 scallions, thinly sliced (green and white portions separated)
- 3 cups cut fresh corn (from 5 ears) or thawed frozen corn (about 1 lb.)
- ½ cup drained, diced roasted red peppers
- ½ tsp. hot chili powder
- ¼ tsp. kosher salt

Make chimichurri:

1 Blend cilantro, garlic, oil and lemon juice and salt in blender until smooth. Transfer to a bowl; set aside.

Make steak:

2 Prepare grill or preheat broiler or grill pan. Season steak with cumin, chili powder, salt and pepper. Cook steak over medium flame, uncovered, for 4 minutes. Turn and cook for 4 more minutes. Transfer to board and let rest for 5 minutes.

Make corn chili:

3 Melt butter in a medium skillet over medium heat, add white of scallions and cook, stirring, for 1 minute. Add corn, red peppers, chili powder and salt; cook, stirring, until corn is crisp-tender, 2 to 3 minutes.

4 Slice steak; arrange on plates. Spoon chili onto plates; sprinkle with green of scallions. Serve with chimichurri.

PER SERVING: Cal. 701, Fat 51g (Sat. 14g), Chol. 100mg, Fiber 5g, Pro. 38g, Carb. 29g, Sod. 1,046mg

CHIMI-WHAT?

Chimichurri sauce is as widely used in Argentina as ketchup is in the U.S. A mixture of olive oil, vinegar and finely chopped parsley, oregano, onion and garlic, chimichurri is a perfect sauce for grilled meat and a common accompaniment to a variety of other dishes, such as empanadas and chorizo (a spicy Spanish sausage).

Sirloin–Snap Pea Stir-Fry

PREP: 10 min. COOK: 15 min. SERVES: 4 COST PER SERVING: **$$$$**

- 1 lb. sugar snap peas
- 3 Tbsp. vegetable oil
- 1 lb. boneless sirloin steak, thinly sliced crosswise
- ¼ cup chopped ginger
- 3 cloves garlic, smashed
- 6 sliced scallions
- 1 cup canned beef broth
- ¼ cup reduced-sodium soy sauce
- 2 Tbsp. cornstarch
- 1 Tbsp. hot sesame oil
- 2 cooked (3 oz.) packages ramen noodles

1 Boil sugar snap peas for 2 minutes, just until they are bright green. Drain, rinse with cold water and set aside.

2 Heat 1 Tbsp. vegetable oil in a skillet over medium-high heat. Add steak and stir-fry for 2 minutes. Transfer to a plate.

3 Add remaining 2 Tbsp. vegetable oil to skillet. Add ginger, garlic and scallions; stir-fry for 1 minute.

4 Stir together beef broth, soy sauce and cornstarch. Add to skillet; stir-fry for 1 minute.

5 Add peas and steak; stir until hot. Stir in sesame oil. Toss ramen noodles and toss until noodles are coated with sauce.

PER SERVING: Cal. 628, Fat 33g (Sat. 10g), Chol. 76mg, Fiber 4g, Pro. 28g, Carb. 54g, Sod. 889mg

LIKE TWO PEAS IN A POD

Sugar snap peas are a cross between the green pea and the snow pea. (You also eat the pods of snow peas, but they're flatter and not as sweet.) You can find sugar snap peas in the freezer section year-round, but from early summer through fall is the time to get them fresh.

Here are a few ways to enjoy snap peas:

Toss snap peas into any summer salad.

Serve them raw with a blue cheese– or sour cream–based dip for an easy appetizer.

Sauté or steam them and toss with pasta, olive oil, lemon zest and pepper for a summer supper.

Grilled Steak with Roasted Potatoes

PREP: **10 min.** MARINATE: **1 hr.** COOK: **20 min.** SERVES: **4** COST PER SERVING: **$$$$**

- 2 lb. flank or skirt steak
- ½ cup olive oil
- 7 cloves garlic, 4 sliced and 3 smashed
- 5 sprigs parsley
- 1½ lb. small red potatoes, quartered
- Salt and ground black pepper

1 Place steak, 6 Tbsp. olive oil, sliced garlic and parsley in a resealable plastic bag, and knead bag to rub ingredients into steak. Let marinate 1 hour at room temperature or overnight in refrigerator.

2 Preheat oven to 450°F. Toss potatoes in a large bowl with remaining 2 Tbsp. olive oil and smashed garlic; season with salt and pepper. Spread potatoes on an oiled baking sheet and roast until golden brown and crisp, about 20 minutes, turning occasionally with a metal spatula.

3 Remove steak from marinade, rubbing off any garlic pieces. Season with salt and pepper. Heat a grill pan over medium-high heat. When hot, brush with oil, add steak and cook for about 7 minutes. Turn and cook for 7 minutes on other side for medium-rare. Transfer steak to a plate, tent with foil to keep warm and let rest for 10 minutes.

4 Thinly slice steak and serve with potatoes and a green vegetable (Green Beans with Lemon and Mint, page 56, are a perfect complement).

PER SERVING: Cal. 560, Fat 28g (Sat. 7g), Chol. 113mg, Fiber 3g, Pro. 50g, Carb. 25g, Sod. 191mg

GRILL INDOORS OR OUT

You can grill this steak in a grill pan or on an outdoor grill. If the steak marinated overnight, remove it from the refrigerator 1 hour before grilling so it can reach room temperature.

Spaghetti and Easy Meatballs

PREP: **10 min.** BAKE: **20 min.** SERVES: **6** COST PER SERVING: **$$**

- ½ cup bread crumbs
- ¼ cup milk
- 1 lb. spaghetti
- 1 (25 oz.) jar tomato sauce
- 1½ lb. ground beef
- ½ cup grated Parmesan
- ½ cup chopped onion
- ¼ cup chopped fresh parsley
- 1 egg, lightly beaten
- 2 cloves garlic, minced
- 1½ tsp. kosher salt

1 Preheat oven to 375°F. Stir together bread crumbs and milk; set aside. Bring a large pot of salted water to a boil. Add spaghetti and cook, stirring often, until al dente, about 10 minutes. Drain well in a colander. In a large, wide saucepan or deep skillet, heat tomato sauce over low heat while you proceed.

2 While pasta is cooking, combine beef, soaked bread crumbs, cheese, onion, parsley, egg, garlic and salt in a large bowl. Form mixture into balls slightly larger than golf balls. (They will shrink as they cook.) Lay meatballs out on two nonstick or oiled baking sheets and bake in oven until nicely browned, about 10 minutes.

3 Transfer meatballs from oven with tongs and place into simmering sauce to combine. Serve meatballs and sauce on top of spaghetti.

PER SERVING: Cal. 754, Fat 35g (Sat. 14g), Chol. 139mg, Fiber 4g, Pro. 36g, Carb. 71g, Sod. 1,315mg

SPAGHETTI SAVVY

Prepare a homemade sauce. Sauté a little onion and garlic, stir in a 6-ounce can of tomato paste and a 28-ounce can of chopped tomatoes. Season and simmer.

Treat meatballs with care. Don't overmix the meat mixture or the meatballs will be tough. You can use a blend of pork, veal and ground beef for more flavor. Add fresh or dried herbs as desired.

Linguine with White Clam Sauce

PREP: 5 min. COOK: 15 min. SERVES: 4 COST PER SERVING: **$$$$**

- ½ lb. linguine
- ¼ cup extra-virgin olive oil
- 4 cloves garlic, smashed
- ½ tsp. crushed red pepper flakes
- 2 dozen littleneck clams
- ½ cup dry white wine
- 1 cup clam juice or chicken broth
- 3 Tbsp. chopped fresh parsley

1 Bring a large saucepan of salted water to a boil; add pasta and cook, stirring often, until al dente. Drain in a colander.

2 Meanwhile, heat olive oil in a large pot over medium-high heat. Add garlic and crushed red pepper and stir until fragrant and golden, 1 to 2 minutes. Add littleneck clams, wine and juice. Cover and cook, stirring occasionally, until clams open, 6 to 8 minutes. (Remove each clam with tongs as it opens and discard those that do not open.) Transfer open clams to each of 4 shallow bowls.

3 Add linguine to clam cooking liquid and toss well. Transfer pasta to each bowl on top of clams. Sprinkle with chopped fresh parsley right before serving.

PER SERVING: Cal. 431, Fat 17g (Sat. 3g), Chol. 68mg, Fiber 1g, Pro. 29g, Carb. 42g, Sod. 488mg

HOW TO CHOOSE CLAMS

Littleneck clams are deliciously plump and juicy. When buying clams, make sure to buy good fresh ones. Look for those with tightly closed, unbroken shells. Don't forget to rinse them with cold water before making this dish. Remember to put a dish for empty clam shells on the table.

Speedy Spaghetti with Chicken and Fresh Tomato

PREP: 10 min. **COOK:** 15 min. **SERVES:** 4 **COST PER SERVING:** **$$**

- 12 oz. uncooked spaghetti
- 2 Tbsp. extra-virgin olive oil
- 1 small onion, finely chopped
- 6 ripe plum tomatoes, seeded and cut in ¼-inch dice
- 12 oz. cooked boneless chicken, torn in pieces (3 cups)
- ½ tsp. salt
- Freshly ground black pepper
- 2 Tbsp. chopped fresh basil
- 1 (4 to 5 oz.) log fresh goat cheese, crumbled

1 Bring a large pot of salted water to a boil, add spaghetti and cook according to package directions, stirring often, until al dente. Reserve 1½ cups cooking liquid from pasta. Drain spaghetti in a colander and reserve.

2 Heat oil over medium heat in same pot. Add onion and cook, stirring, until softened, about 5 minutes. Return pasta to pot along with tomato, chicken and pasta liquid. Toss well and season with salt and pepper to taste.

3 Transfer pasta to plates. Sprinkle with basil, dot with goat cheese and serve immediately.

PER SERVING: Cal. 642, Fat 21g (Sat. 7g), Chol. 89mg, Fiber 4g, Pro. 42g, Carb. 70g, Sod. 480mg

PASTA POINTERS

Add more cheese. If you love cheese or prefer not to use chicken, double the goat cheese.

Prevent sticking. Use plenty of water and stir pasta frequently to keep it from sticking together. Make sure that the pasta is submerged the whole time.

Make it al dente. When pasta is prepared al dente, it is tender but firm. If it's undercooked, pasta is slightly crunchy; when it's overcooked, it is limp and soggy. Test whether the pasta is ready before draining it.

Penne with Sweet Peas and Prosciutto

PREP: **10** min.   COOK: **15** min.   SERVES: **6**   COST PER SERVING: **$**

- 1 lb. penne pasta
- 1 Tbsp. olive oil
- 6 Tbsp. unsalted butter
- 1 onion, chopped
- 4 oz. thinly sliced prosciutto, halved lengthwise and cut into ½-inch strips
- 1 (10 oz.) package frozen peas, thawed
- 1 cup grated Parmesan, plus more for serving
- 1 tsp. kosher salt
- ¼ tsp. black pepper
- 1 tsp. grated lemon peel

1 In a large pot of boiling salted water, cook pasta until al dente, about 12 minutes. Drain thoroughly and return to pot. Toss pasta with oil.

2 While pasta is cooking, heat 1 Tbsp. butter in a large nonstick skillet over medium heat. Add onion and cook, stirring, until it's translucent, 5 minutes. Add prosciutto and cook for 2 minutes. Add peas and cook for 3 minutes.

3 Toss mixture with pasta in pot, along with remaining 5 Tbsp. butter, Parmesan, salt, pepper and lemon peel. Heat through.

4 Serve pasta with more cheese if desired.

PER SERVING: Cal. 541, Fat 24g (Sat. 13g), Chol. 55mg, Fiber 10g, Pro. 25g, Carb. 54g, Sod. 1,142mg

Pasta and Bean Soup with Cheese Toasts

PREP: 5 min. COOK: 20 min. SERVES: 4 COST PER SERVING: $$

For soup:

- 2 cups ditalini or small pasta shells
- 2 Tbsp. extra-virgin olive oil
- 1 medium onion, finely chopped
- 1 clove garlic, lightly crushed
- 3 cups tomato sauce
- 2 cups low-sodium vegetable broth or chicken broth
- 1 (10 oz.) package frozen broccoli florets, thawed and chopped
- 1 (10 oz.) package frozen peas
- 1 (15 oz.) can chickpeas (garbanzo beans), drained and rinsed

For cheese toasts:

- 4 1-inch-thick slices Italian bread
- 2 Tbsp. olive oil
- ½ cup grated Parmesan cheese

Make soup:

1 Fill a large pot with salted water and bring to a boil over high heat. Add pasta and cook, stirring often, until al dente, about 10 minutes. Drain in a colander.

2 Heat oil in a large saucepan over medium heat. Add onion and garlic and cook, stirring often, until softened, about 5 minutes. Stir in tomato sauce, broth, broccoli, peas and chickpeas. Bring to a boil. Cover, reduce heat and simmer gently for 10 minutes. Just before serving, stir in pasta.

Make cheese toasts:

3 Preheat broiler. Brush bread slices with oil and broil until golden, about 3 minutes. Sprinkle with Parmesan and broil until bubbling, about 3 minutes more. Serve soup with cheese toasts.

PER SERVING: Cal. 372, Fat 9g (Sat. 1g), Chol. 0mg, Fiber 13g, Pro. 17g, Carb. 57g, Sod. 1,169mg

TOMATO SAUCE TIPS

Cook tomato sauce with a few choice ingredients and serve over pasta for an easy and satisfying meal. You'll need about 2½ cups of sauce to coat a pound (uncooked) of pasta.

Stir ¾ cup half-and-half and chopped basil or parsley into sauce; heat. Serve over pasta with grated Parmesan cheese.

Cook 1 pound Italian sausage in a skillet until browned; stir in sauce and chopped fresh or dried rosemary.

Stir in chili powder to taste, 1 (16-oz.) can black beans and 1 cup corn. Serve over pasta and top with Cheddar cheese.

Rice Noodles with Beef

PREP: **20 min.** COOK: **10 min.** SERVES: **6** COST PER SERVING: **$$**

- 1 (8 oz.) package pad Thai rice-stick noodles
- 1 (1 lb.) bag frozen Asian stir-fry vegetables
- 2 cloves garlic, minced
- 1-inch piece fresh ginger, peeled and grated
- 1½ Tbsp. soy sauce
- 1 Tbsp. red curry paste
- 1 Tbsp. rice wine vinegar
- 2 Tbsp. fresh lime juice
- 5 Tbsp. peanut oil
- 1 lb. beef sirloin or flank steak, sliced ¼-inch thick
- 1 red bell pepper, sliced into ¼-inch strips
- 6 scallions, sliced (1 cup)
- ½ lb. bean sprouts (2 cups), optional
- ½ cup roasted, unsalted peanuts, chopped (3 oz.), optional

1 Soak rice noodles in cold water for 15 minutes; drain. Add to a pot of boiling water and cook for 5 minutes. Drain again and set aside.

2 Rinse Asian vegetables in a colander briefly with cold water; let drain thoroughly. In a small bowl, stir together garlic, ginger, soy sauce, curry paste, vinegar, lime juice and 2 Tbsp. peanut oil; set aside.

3 Heat 1 Tbsp. peanut oil in a large nonstick skillet or wok over medium-high heat. Add half of beef and stir-fry for 4 minutes. Transfer to a plate. Repeat process with 1 Tbsp. oil and remaining beef. Keep beef warm. Wipe out pan; add remaining 1 Tbsp. oil and red pepper, then stir-fry for 2 minutes. Add scallions and reserved Asian vegetables and cook for 3 minutes.

4 Add reserved sauce to skillet; cook for 1 minute. Add beef and cooked noodles and toss thoroughly to combine with sauce.

5 Serve noodles in bowls with bean sprouts and peanuts, if desired.

PER SERVING: Cal. 380, Fat 15g (Sat. 3g), Chol. 46mg, Fiber 2g, Pro. 21g, Carb. 40g, Sod. 378mg

Grilled Pizza with Onions and Prosciutto

PREP: **20 min.** COOK: **14 min.** SERVES: **4** COST PER SERVING: **$$$**

- **1 lb. packaged frozen pizza dough, thawed**
- **⅓ cup olive oil**
- **1 large sweet onion (14 oz.), such as Vidalia or Walla Walla, trimmed and halved, with roots intact**
- **½ cup crème fraîche**
- **⅛ tsp. salt**
- **2 oz. paper-thin sliced prosciutto, preferably imported, torn into 1-inch strips**
- **¾ cup small fresh basil leaves**

1 Prepare grill. Place dough on work surface, knead in 1 Tbsp. olive oil and shape into 2 balls. Cover with a towel and let rest for 10 minutes.

2 Slice onion in half, then slice each half into thin wedges, leaving root end intact. Brush top and bottom lightly with oil. Grill onion, turning once, until charred and just tender, about 3 minutes. Transfer to a plate and reserve.

3 Roll out and stretch 1 dough ball to ½ inch thick. Place on a greased baking sheet and brush top of dough lightly with oil. Place on grill oil-side down. Brush dough with oil, cover and cook until bottom is crisp, about 4 minutes; flip, cover and cook until crisp on both sides and cooked through, about 4 minutes.

4 Transfer pizza to a board. Stir together crème fraîche and salt and spread half on grilled dough. Repeat with remaining dough and crème fraîche mixture. Cut root end from onion, then sprinkle over the crème fraîche mixture, Top with prosciutto and basil. Cut each pizza into 4 slices and serve.

PER SERVING: Cal. 587, Fat 40g (Sat. 14g), Chol. 41mg, Fiber 4g, Pro. 13g, Carb. 54g, Sod. 835mg

THE EVER-RELIABLE ONION

Onions add zing and crunch to a virtually limitless range of dishes. But did you know that these familiar vegetables come in two categories?

Fall-winter "storage" onions have several layers of thick skin, less liquid and will keep longer. Choose onions that are heavy for their size but don't have a strong scent.

Spring-summer "fresh" onions have a limited shelf life and a sweeter, more delicate taste.

Bacon and Tomato Pasta Salad

PREP: **10 min.** COOK: **20 min.** SERVES: **6** COST PER SERVING: **$$**

- 1 lb. orecchiette pasta
- 1 (1 lb.) package smoked bacon, cut crosswise into ½-inch slices
- 2 Tbsp. olive oil
- 4 ears fresh corn, kernels removed from ears, or 1 (1 lb.) package frozen corn, thawed
- 2 (10 oz.) packages grape tomatoes, halved lengthwise
- 2 Tbsp. red wine vinegar
- Salt and ground black pepper
- ¾ cup chopped fresh basil leaves

1 Fill a large pot with salted water and bring to a boil over high heat. Add pasta and cook, stirring occasionally, until al dente, about 10 minutes. Drain and set aside.

2 Meanwhile, place bacon in a large skillet over medium-high heat and cook until crisp and browned, about 12 minutes. Using a slotted spoon, transfer bacon to paper towels to drain.

3 Discard all but 2 Tbsp. bacon fat and reduce heat to medium. Add olive oil. When it's hot, add corn and cook for 3 to 4 minutes (1 to 2 minutes if corn was frozen). Add tomatoes and cook until just softened, 1 to 2 minutes. Stir in vinegar. Remove from heat.

4 Return pasta to large pot and add bacon and vegetables. Season with salt and pepper. Toss gently to combine. Warm over medium-low heat for 2 minutes. Toss with basil just before serving.

PER SERVING: Cal. 548, Fat 22g (Sat. 6g), Chol. 23mg, Fiber 6g, Pro. 19g, Carb. 72g, Sod. 356mg

QUICK BASIL PESTO

Fresh basil is available year-round, but summer is the time when its true flavor really shines. To use up any extra basil, make pesto.

A perfect alternative to traditional red sauce, pesto is also delicious in salads and sandwiches, or spooned on top of soups. If you plan to store pesto, top it with a very thin layer of olive oil to keep it from turning brown. Store pesto in the refrigerator for up to 2 weeks. (True pesto contains pine nuts and Parmagiano-Reggiano cheese, but our version keeps longer and is lower in fat.)

1 Mince 1 large clove garlic in a food processor.

2 Add 2 packed cups (washed and spun dry) fresh basil leaves and process to chop.

3 With motor running, drizzle in ⅔ cup extra-virgin olive oil. Season with ½ tsp. salt.

Asian Chicken and Rice Noodle Salad

PREP: 20 min. COOK: 5 min. SERVES: 4 COST PER SERVING: $$

The dressing:

- ¼ cup Thai or Vietnamese fish sauce
- ¼ cup sugar
- 3 Tbsp. fresh lime juice
- 1 clove garlic, minced
- ¼ tsp. crushed red pepper flakes
- ¾ cup warm water

The salad:

- 8 oz. rice noodles
- 3 cups diced cooked chicken (about 10 oz.)
- 1 cup mung bean sprouts
- 4 scallions, thinly sliced
- 1 carrot, peeled and grated
- ¼ cup chopped fresh cilantro leaves
- ⅓ cup chopped unsalted dry-roasted peanuts (optional)

Make the dressing:

1 Whisk together fish sauce, sugar, lime juice, garlic, red pepper flakes. Stir in water and set aside.

Make the salad:

2 Place noodles in a large bowl in sink; cover them with hot water and let stand for 10 minutes. Meanwhile, bring a large pot of water to a boil. Drain noodles and add to pot; cook, stirring, until tender, 3 to 4 minutes. Drain and rinse with cold water until cool.

3 Transfer noodles to a large salad bowl. Add chicken and remaining ingredients; toss well. Pour half of dressing on salad and toss again. Add more dressing as desired.

PER SERVING: Cal. 486, Fat 8g (Sat. 2g), Chol. 93mg, Fiber 2g, Pro. 35g, Carb. 66g, Sod. 1,596mg

Flank Steak and Watercress Salad

PREP: **10 min.** STAND: **5 min.** COOK: **12 min.** SERVES: **4** COST PER SERVING: **$$$**

- 1 (1½ lb.) trimmed flank steak
- 1 tsp. salt
- ½ tsp. ground black pepper
- 10 oz. watercress, tough stems discarded
- 1 cup grape tomatoes, halved
- 4 radishes, trimmed and thinly sliced
- 2½ Tbsp. extra-virgin olive oil
- 2 tsp. red wine vinegar
- 3 oz. (¾ cup) blue cheese, crumbled (optional)

WHAT, NO WATERCRESS?

Watercress should be widely available in the springtime, but if you can't find it in your local grocery store, substitute baby arugula for an equally spicy flavor, or use mixed baby greens.

1 Preheat a large grill pan over medium heat. Sprinkle steak on both sides with ¾ tsp. salt and ¼ tsp. pepper. Make sure pan is hot, then cook steak for about 6 minutes per side, turning once, for medium-rare. Transfer to a cutting board, cover loosely with foil and let stand for 5 minutes.

2 Combine watercress, tomatoes and radishes in a large bowl. Drizzle oil and vinegar on top; toss well. Season with remaining ¼ tsp. each of salt and pepper, then toss again.

3 Thinly slice steak and divide among 4 dinner plates. Top each portion with salad. Sprinkle blue cheese on top, if desired.

PER SERVING: Cal. 431, Fat 28g (Sat. 11g), Chol. 100mg, Fiber 2g, Pro. 41g, Carb. 4g, Sod. 1,021mg

Grilled Shrimp and Arugula Salad

PREP: **10 min.**   GRILL: **10 min.**   SERVES: **4**   COST PER SERVING: **$$$**

- 1 lb. medium shrimp, peeled
- ¼ cup olive oil
- 6 slices crusty Italian bread
- 1 large clove garlic, peeled
- 1 tsp. balsamic vinegar
- 1 tsp. finely grated fresh lemon peel
- ½ tsp. kosher salt
- 1 bunch arugula (about 3 oz.), washed and dried
- 3 medium tomatoes, cut into wedges and halved
- Ground black pepper

1 Prepare grill. Toss shrimp with 1 Tbsp. oil. Transfer to grill and cook, turning, until charred and firm, about 5 minutes. Transfer cooked shrimp to a large salad bowl.

2 Brush bread with remaining oil and then grill, turning it occasionally, until toasted on both sides, about 5 minutes. Rub toast slices with garlic clove. Transfer toast to a board and cut into cubes; add cubes to bowl with shrimp, followed by vinegar, lemon peel and salt. Toss mixture well. Add arugula and tomato, season with pepper, and toss again.

PER SERVING: Cal. 390, Fat 18g (Sat. 3g), Chol. 172mg, Fiber 3g, Pro. 28g, Carb. 29g, Sod. 560mg

Mashed Potato Gratin page 62

Roasted Peppers with Black Olives page 58

Louisiana Sweet Potato Salad page 66

Roasted Broccoli
with Orange Hollandaise Sauce page 57

Side Dishes

A meal is only as good as its side dishes, and in this chapter we give you 19 delectable sides that are good enough for star billing on any plate!

No summer barbecue is complete without **Tomato Succotash** (page 61); a chilly night will be made that much warmer with a helping of **Roasted Winter Vegetables** (page 59). And **Tennessee Buttermilk Biscuits** (page 71) are a perfect addition to any table, whether it's a weekend breakfast or a weeknight dinner.

SUPER-FAST SIDES

Pressed for time? Try one of these quick (ready in less than 15 minutes!) sides:

Mushroom-Scallion Salad: Whisk ¼ cup red wine vinegar, 2 minced shallots, 1½ tsp. ground coriander, ¾ tsp. kosher salt and ¼ tsp. ground black pepper in a medium bowl. Whisk in ½ cup olive oil. Stir in 1 (10 oz.) package of small white sliced mushrooms and 4 thinly sliced scallions.

Zesty Spring Peas: In a large skillet, melt 3 Tbsp. butter over medium heat. Add 5 chopped scallions and cook, stirring, until softened, 3 minutes. Stir in 1 tsp. grated fresh orange zest and salt and pepper to taste. Increase heat to medium-high, add 3 (10 oz.) packages frozen baby peas and cook, stirring, until heated through, about 5 minutes.

Cheddar Biscuits page 70

Green Beans with Lemon and Mint

PREP: 10 min.　COOK: 10 min.　SERVES: 8　COST PER SERVING: **$$**

- 1 lb. fresh green beans
- ¼ cup flat-leaf parsley leaves
- ¼ cup fresh mint leaves
- 1 tsp. grated fresh lemon zest
- 2 Tbsp. fresh lemon juice
- 2 Tbsp. olive oil
- 1 tsp. kosher salt
- ¼ tsp. ground black pepper

1 In a large pot of boiling salted water, cook beans until crisp-tender, about 5 minutes. Drain and refresh under cold water. Pat dry.

2 Chop parsley, mint and lemon zest. Put in a bowl and stir in lemon juice. Heat oil in a large, deep skillet over medium-high heat. Add beans, parsley mixture and salt and pepper; cook until just heated through, about 5 minutes. Serve hot.

PER SERVING: Cal. 50, Fat 4g (Sat. 1g), Chol. 0mg, Fiber 2g, Pro. 1g, Carb. 5g, Sod. 240mg

Roasted Asparagus

PREP: 4 min.　COOK: 15 min.　SERVES: 8　COST PER SERVING: **$**

- 2 lb. asparagus, ends trimmed
- 2 Tbsp. extra-virgin olive oil
- ½ tsp. kosher salt
- ¼ tsp. ground black pepper
- 2 medium oranges, cut into slices for garnish

1 Preheat oven to 450°F. Line a baking sheet with parchment paper or foil. Arrange asparagus in a single layer. Drizzle oil on top and sprinkle with salt and pepper.

2 Roast until crisp-tender, about 15 minutes. (Add or subtract approximately 5 minutes for thicker or thinner asparagus.) Serve warm or at room temperature with orange wedges to garnish.

PER SERVING: Cal. 72, Fat 4g (Sat. 0g), Chol. 0mg, Fiber 3g, Pro. 3g, Carb. 9g, Sod. 120mg

Roasted Broccoli with Orange Hollandaise Sauce

PREP: 15 min. ROAST: 10 min. SERVES: 8 COST PER SERVING: ¢

- 2 (1 lb.) bunches broccoli, cut into florets; stems peeled and sliced crosswise, ¼-inch thick
- 2 Tbsp. extra-virgin olive oil
- ¼ tsp. salt
- Ground black pepper, to taste
- 4 cloves garlic, thinly sliced
- Orange Hollandaise Sauce, for serving (see recipe, right)

1 Place rack in upper third of oven and preheat oven to 500°F. Line a large baking sheet with aluminum foil.

2 Rinse broccoli, but do not dry. Place in a large mixing bowl, drizzle with olive oil and sprinkle with salt and pepper; toss well to coat thoroughly. Spread broccoli in an even layer on prepared baking sheet. Distribute garlic on top of broccoli and roast about 10 minutes, until crisp-tender and lightly charred in spots. Serve warm or at room temperature.

PER SERVING: Cal. 64, Fat 4g (Sat. 1g), Chol. 0mg, Fiber 3g, Pro. 4g, Carb. 6g, Sod. 90mg

ORANGE HOLLANDAISE SAUCE

Boil 6 Tbsp. fresh orange juice until reduced by half. Transfer to a blender; add 1 Tbsp. lemon juice and 6 egg yolks and then blend. With machine on, drizzle in ¼ cup boiling water. Gradually add 2 sticks hot, melted, unsalted butter, then ½ tsp. finely grated orange peel, ¾ tsp. kosher salt and ¼ tsp. pepper, blending until sauce thickens. Transfer to a double boiler. Whisk until sauce becomes even thicker and is hot.

PER SERVING: Cal. 226, Fat 24g (Sat. 14g), Chol. 197mg, Fiber 0g, Pro. 2g, Carb. 2g, Sod. 164mg

Roasted Peppers with Black Olives

PREP: 30 min. COOK: 25 min. STAND: 1 hr. SERVES: 8 COST PER SERVING: **$$**

- 3 orange bell peppers
- 3 red bell peppers
- 3 yellow bell peppers
- 3 Tbsp. olive oil, preferably extra-virgin
- 1 Tbsp. red wine vinegar
- 1 small clove garlic, chopped
- Salt and ground black pepper
- 8 pitted black Mediterranean-style olives
- 20 small leaves fresh mint

1 Broil peppers 4 to 5 inches below heat source, turning every 5 minutes, until skins are blackened, about 25 minutes. Transfer to a large bowl, cover with a large plate or plastic wrap and let steam until cool enough to handle. Peel peppers, trim, discard seeds and ribs and cut lengthwise into ½-inch-wide strips.

2 Toss together peppers, oil, vinegar and garlic in a serving bowl; season with salt and pepper. Let stand at least 1 hour before serving. (Salad can be refrigerated, tightly wrapped, for up to 3 days.)

3 Just before serving, toss olives with peppers. Sprinkle salad with mint and serve at room temperature.

PER SERVING: Cal. 96, Fat 7g (Sat. 1g), Chol. 0mg, Fiber 3g, Pro. 1g, Carb. 9g, Sod. 58mg

CHOOSE YOUR OLIVES

Greek kalamatas, Italian Gaetas and French Niçoise olives are all good choices for this salad. You can use dry-cured (black and wrinkled) or brine-cured (purple and smooth) varieties.

Roasted Winter Vegetables

PREP: 15 min. ROAST: 20 min. SERVES: 6 COST PER SERVING: ¢

- 1 lb. parsnips, peeled and cut into thick sticks
- 1 lb. carrots, peeled and cut into thick sticks
- 1 (10 oz.) package frozen pearl onions, thawed
- 8 oz. brussels sprouts, halved
- 6 garlic cloves, smashed with the side of a knife and peeled
- 3 Tbsp. olive oil
- Leaves from 1 sprig fresh rosemary (or 1 tsp. dried rosemary)
- ½ tsp. kosher salt
- ¼ tsp. ground black pepper

1 Preheat oven to 500°F.

2 Combine parsnips, carrots, onions, brussels sprouts and garlic on a large rimmed baking sheet lined with foil.

3 Sprinkle vegetables with olive oil and toss with rosemary, salt and pepper until coated. Spread vegetables evenly into a single layer on the baking sheet. Roast until tender and browned on edges, about 25 minutes.

PER SERVING: Cal. 187, Fat 8g (Sat. 0g), Chol. 0mg, Fiber 8g, Pro. 4g, Carb. 30g, Sod. 206mg

COOKING WINTER SQUASH

Another delightful winter vegetable is winter squash. Widely available varieties are acorn, butternut, hubbard and turban. Peak season for winter squash is October through December. Choose squash that are heavy for their size and have deeply colored, blemish-free rinds.

Roasted squash: Halve squash lengthwise and scoop out seeds. Peel with a vegetable peeler and cut into 2-inch wedges. Spread in a roasting pan, toss with oil and seasonings and roast at 450°F for about 45 minutes.

Baked squash: Bake halved and seeded squash cut side down for 45 to 60 minutes at 350°F; turn upright, brush with butter, honey, maple syrup or jelly and sprinkle with spices or herbs.

Pureed squash: Pierce a small, whole squash with a fork, rub with oil and bake at 350°F until tender, about 1 hour. Split open, scoop out flesh into a food processor and puree with butter or cream and seasonings.

Okra Stewed with Tomatoes

PREP: 10 min. COOK: 35 min. SERVES: 4 COST PER SERVING: ¢

- 1 Tbsp. vegetable oil
- 1 large onion, chopped
- ½ tsp. salt, plus more to taste
- 1 lb. okra, trimmed and cut into ¾-inch pieces
- 1 (28 oz.) can diced tomatoes in juice
- Ground black pepper to taste

1 Heat oil in a large saucepan over medium-low heat.

2 Add onion and salt and cook, stirring occasionally, until soft, about 10 minutes. Add okra and tomatoes; bring to a boil.

3 Reduce heat to maintain a simmer and cook until okra is tender, about 25 minutes. Season with salt and pepper to taste.

PER SERVING: Cal. 59, Fat 2g (Sat. 0g), Chol. 0mg, Fiber 3g, Pro. 2g, Carb. 10g, Sod. 415mg

Creamed Peas and Pearl Onions

PREP: 5 min. COOK: 15 min. SERVES: 8 COST PER SERVING: ¢

- 3 Tbsp. unsalted butter
- ¼ tsp. dried thyme
- 3 Tbsp. all-purpose flour
- 2 cups whole milk, warmed
- 2 (10 oz.) bags frozen pearl onions, thawed
- 1 (10 oz.) package frozen tiny green peas, thawed
- ¼ tsp. kosher salt
- ⅛ tsp. ground black pepper

1 Melt butter with thyme in a large saucepan over medium heat.

2 Add flour and cook, whisking, for 2 minutes. Slowly add warm milk, whisking constantly, and cook until mixture thickens and comes to a boil.

3 Reduce heat to low and simmer, whisking, 3 minutes. Stir in onions, peas, salt and pepper, and cook until heated through, about 7 minutes.

PER SERVING: Cal. 139, Fat 7g (Sat. 4g), Chol. 20mg, Fiber 3g, Pro. 5g, Carb. 16g, Sod. 140mg

Mashed Potatoes with Onions

PREP: 12 min. COOK: 20 min. SERVES: 8 COST PER SERVING: ¢

- 3 lb. baking potatoes, peeled and cut into 1-inch chunks
- 2 Tbsp. olive oil
- 1 medium onion, quartered lengthwise and thinly sliced
- 1½ tsp. kosher salt
- ½ tsp. ground black pepper
- ½ cup milk
- ½ cup sour cream

1 Place potatoes in a large pot and add cold water to cover. Add salt and bring to a boil. Reduce heat and simmer until potatoes are tender, 15 to 20 minutes. Remove from heat, drain potatoes well in a colander and return potatoes to pot.

2 Meanwhile, heat oil in a large cast-iron skillet over medium-high heat until hot. Add onion and cook, stirring occasionally, until it begins to brown, about 4 minutes; reduce heat to medium-low and cook, stirring, until onion is very soft, about 8 minutes more; set aside.

3 Mash warm potatoes with a masher until coarse. Add salt, pepper and milk; mash until desired consistency. Gently stir in sour cream and caramelized onion until combined.

PER SERVING: Cal. 193, Fat 8g (Sat. 3g), Chol. 12mg, Fiber 4g, Pro. 4g, Carb. 27g, Sod. 391mg

Tomato Succotash

PREP: 10 min. COOK: 20 min. SERVES: 12 COST PER SERVING: ¢

- 2 (10 oz.) packages frozen baby lima beans
- ¼ cup vegetable oil
- 3 stalks celery, chopped
- 2 small red onions, chopped
- 3 large, ripe tomatoes, cored, seeded and chopped
- 1 cup fresh or frozen corn kernels
- ¼ cup cider vinegar
- Salt and ground black pepper
- ½ cup chopped basil

1 Cook lima beans in 1 cup boiling water for 10 minutes; rinse and drain.

2 In skillet, heat oil over medium heat. Add celery and onions; cook for 4 minutes. Add lima beans, tomatoes, corn and vinegar; season with salt and pepper. Cook for 2 minutes. Toss with basil.

PER SERVING: Cal. 122, Fat 5g (Sat. 1g), Chol. 0mg, Fiber 4g, Pro. 4g, Carb. 16g, Sod. 16mg

Mashed Potato Gratin

PREP: 20 min. BAKE: 35 min. SERVES: 8 COST PER SERVING: ¢

- 3 lb. baking potatoes, peeled and cut into 1-inch chunks
- 2 cloves garlic, peeled
- Kosher salt
- ½ cup heavy cream, at room temperature
- ¼ cup snipped fresh chives
- 4 Tbsp. unsalted butter, at room temperature
- Ground black pepper
- ½ cup (1 oz.) finely grated Parmesan cheese

1 Place potatoes and garlic in a large saucepan and cover with cool water. Season with salt and bring water to a boil over high heat. Reduce heat to low, cover saucepan and simmer until potatoes are tender when pierced with a fork, about 15 minutes.

2 Drain potatoes and garlic and return to pot. Heat over high heat, shaking pan, until any liquid has evaporated, about 30 seconds. Mash potatoes and garlic until smooth. Add cream, chives and butter; season with salt and pepper. Transfer potato mixture to a shallow 2-quart flameproof baking dish. (The gratin can be prepared to this point up to 5 hours ahead. Cover and keep at room temperature.)

3 Preheat broiler. Sprinkle potatoes with Parmesan. Broil gratin 2 inches from heat, rotating pan if necessary, until golden, crusty and heated through, 5 to 7 minutes.

PER SERVING: Cal. 238, Fat 13g (Sat. 8g), Chol. 39mg, Fiber 1g, Pro. 6g, Carb. 25g, Sod. 333mg

CUT YOUR COOKING TIME

When you're boiling potatoes—for mashed potatoes, potato salad or any other potato dish—cut the potatoes into very small pieces to reduce the amount of time it will take for them to cook.

Ginger–Sweet Potato Mash

PREP: 15 min.   COOK: 25 min.   SERVES: 8   COST PER SERVING: $

- 3 lb. sweet potatoes, peeled and cut into 1-inch chunks
- 1 piece fresh ginger, peeled (about 1 Tbsp.)
- 2 Tbsp. unsalted butter
- 2 Tbsp. honey
- ¼ tso. salt
- ¼ tsp. ground black pepper
- ¼ cup heavy cream

1 Place potatoes in a large saucepan with cold, salted water to cover. Bring to a boil, reduce heat and simmer until potatoes are tender, about 15 minutes.

2 Drain well; return potatoes to pot. Mash well. Finely grate ginger and squeeze over potatoes to extract juice; discard ginger. Add butter, honey, ½ tsp. salt and ¼ tsp. pepper; mash again. Add cream and beat with a wooden spoon until blended.

PER SERVING: Cal. 246, Fat 6g (Sat. 4g), Chol. 18mg, Fiber 5g, Pro. 3g, Carb. 46g, Sod. 143mg

HOW TO CHOOSE & STORE SWEET POTATOES

This winter, take a trip to your local market and bring back sweet potatoes for the next family dinner or holiday meal. These large roots (often mislabeled yams) are available all year, but they're sweetest in the fall and winter. So get in the kitchen and start cooking this Thanksgiving staple.

Pick them. Sweet potatoes vary in size and shape. Choose those that are very firm and smooth and have no areas of softening, sprouting or blackening.

Store them. Do not refrigerate. They will lose their sweetness since their natural sugars will convert to starch. Store in a dry, dark place.

Corn Pudding

PREP: 10 min. BAKE: 1 hr. SERVES: 6 COST PER SERVING: ¢

- 1 Tbsp. unsalted butter, for greasing casserole
- 4 large eggs
- ¾ cup heavy cream
- ¾ cup milk
- 3 cups white corn (from about 6 medium ears)
- 1 Tbsp. finely chopped fresh chives
- Pinch of ground nutmeg
- 1 tsp. salt
- Pinch of white pepper

1 Preheat oven to 325ºF. Grease a shallow 1½-quart casserole dish with butter.

2 Whisk together eggs, cream and milk in a medium bowl. Add corn, chives, nutmeg, salt and white pepper; stir mixture to combine. Pour into casserole dish.

3 Place casserole dish in large roasting pan and pour hot water to reach halfway up sides of casserole. Bake 45 minutes to 1 hour. Remove casserole from water bath and let cool for 10 minutes.

PER SERVING: Cal. 245, Fat. 18g (Sat. 10g), Chol. 194mg, Fiber 1g, Pro. 8g, Carb. 17g, Sod. 456mg

HOW TO CHOOSE & USE CORN

Corn comes in a range of colors, from almost white to deep yellow. Which is your favorite?

Yellow corn has large, bright yellow kernels bursting with flavor. This sweet and succulent corn is also known as Golden Bantam.

White corn, also known as Country Gentleman, has smaller, sweeter white kernels that may be arranged irregularly, not in neat rows.

Butter and sugar corn is a popular hybrid. As its name indicates, this hybrid has alternating golden yellow and creamy white kernels.

Baby corn has entirely edible, tender ears. Popular in Thai and Chinese cuisines, baby corn can often be purchased in jars or cans.

Louisiana Sweet Potato Salad

PREP: 15 min. COOK: 15 min. SERVES: 8 COST PER SERVING: **$$**

- 3 lb. medium sweet potatoes, peeled and cut into 1-inch pieces
- 2 stalks celery, thinly sliced
- ⅓ cup finely diced red onion
- ¼ cup chopped celery leaves
- 1 Tbsp. thinly sliced, long hot red peppers
- ¼ cup Southeast Vinegar Splash (see recipe, below)
- 1 Tbsp. fresh lime juice
- 1 Tbsp. ketchup
- 1 tsp. minced garlic
- 1 tsp. mustard
- ⅔ cup olive oil
- ½ tsp. salt
- ¼ tsp. ground black pepper
- ⅓ cup chopped, toasted pecans

1 Bring a pot of salted water to a boil. Add potatoes; simmer until tender.

2 Drain cooked potatoes under cold running water. Transfer to a bowl. Add celery, onion, celery leaves and hot pepper; toss. Whisk Southeast Vinegar Splash with lime juice, ketchup, garlic, mustard, olive oil, salt and pepper; drizzle over salad and toss. Sprinkle pecans on top.

PER SERVING: Cal. 388, Fat 23g (Sat. 3g), Chol. 0mg, Fiber 6g, Pro. 4g, Carb. 46g, Sod. 286mg

ADD SOUTHERN FLAVOR

Add a light coating of these sauces to cooked meat to add the right touch.

Southeast Vinegar Splash

Whisk together 2 cups cider vinegar, ½ cup light brown sugar, ⅓ cup ketchup, ½ Tbsp. salt, 1 Tbsp. Better-than-Basic Barbecue Rub (see recipe below) and ½ tsp. crushed red pepper flakes. Continue to whisk until sugar dissolves. Store in a glass jar in refrigerator.

Better-than-Basic Barbecue Rub

In a small bowl, stir together ½ cup sugar, 6 Tbsp. kosher salt, ¼ cup sweet paprika, 2 Tbsp. hot paprika, 2 Tbsp. chili powder, 1 Tbsp. dry mustard, ½ tsp. cayenne and ½ tsp. black pepper until well blended. Store in a glass jar up for to 6 months.

Summer Vegetable Bow-Tie Salad

PREP: 45 min. **GRILL:** 12 min. **SERVES:** 8 **COST PER SERVING:** $$

- 5 slender Italian eggplants (about 1 lb.), trimmed
- Kosher salt
- 3 small zucchini (1 lb.), ends trimmed
- 2 medium yellow summer squash (1 lb.), ends trimmed
- 1 cup extra-virgin olive oil
- 3 medium tomatoes, seeded and diced into ½-inch pieces
- 1 lb. farfalle pasta
- 1 cup lightly packed fresh basil leaves
- 1 tsp. finely grated fresh lemon peel
- 1 Tbsp. fresh lemon juice
- Ground black pepper

1 Prepare grill. Slice eggplant lengthwise into ½-inch thick slices. Arrange slices in a single layer in a colander in the sink; sprinkle with salt. Repeat layering and salting with remaining slices and let stand for 15 minutes.

2 Slice zucchini and squash lengthwise, into ½-inch thick slices. Brush slices lightly on both sides with oil; grill over medium flame, covered, until charred and tender, about 6 minutes, turning once.

3 Rinse eggplant slices with cold water and pat dry. Brush lightly with oil; grill, covered, until charred and tender, about 6 minutes, turning once. Cut grilled vegetable slices into ½- to ⅓-inch dice and transfer to a large bowl. Add tomatoes and toss well.

4 Cook farfalle just until al dente according to package instructions. Drain; rinse with cold water until cold; add to bowl.

5 Combine basil, lemon peel and juice, salt, pepper and 1 cup olive oil in a blender and blend until smooth. Pour over pasta; toss well. Serve this dish at room temperature.

PER SERVING: Cal. 476, Fat 30g (Sat. 4g), Chol. 0mg, Fiber 10g, Pro. 11g, Carb. 44g, Sod. 371mg

PASTA SALAD SECRETS

Store leftover pasta. Refrigerate extra plain cooked pasta in an airtight container for 3 to 5 days. Mix with a splash of oil to keep it from sticking together.

Stock up on dry pasta. It will keep in your cupboard for up to a year.

Keep tomatoes fresh. Don't put tomatoes in the refrigerator—it ruins their flavor and texture. Instead, keep them on the kitchen counter, away from sunlight.

Harvest Sausage and Fruit Stuffing

PREP: 20 min. BAKE: 45 min. SERVES: 8 COST PER SERVING: ¢

- 1 lb. sliced soft white bread
- ½ lb. sliced soft whole wheat bread
- 10 oz. breakfast sausage meat or sweet Italian sausage, removed from casings
- 1 Tbsp. unsalted butter
- 1 medium onion, chopped
- 2 stalks celery, finely diced
- ¾ tsp. kosher salt
- ¼ tsp. ground black pepper
- 1 Golden Delicious apple, cored and cut into ½-inch dice
- 1 ripe Bartlett pear, cored and cut into ½-inch dice
- ½ tsp. dried thyme
- 1 cup chicken broth
- ½ cup cranberry-raspberry juice

1 Preheat oven to 400°F. Tear white and whole wheat breads into medium-size pieces and put in a large bowl.

2 Put sausage meat in a skillet and place over medium heat; break up meat with a wooden spoon and cook, stirring, until meat is nicely browned and somewhat crumbly, 6 to 8 minutes. Use a slotted spoon to transfer sausage to bowl with bread. Add butter, onion and celery to sausage drippings in skillet. Season with kosher salt and pepper and cook, stirring often, for 5 minutes. Add to sausage and bread along with apple, pear and thyme; toss well. Add chicken broth and fruit juice and toss again to combine.

3 Transfer stuffing to a 13-by-9-inch baking dish or other shallow, 3-quart baking dish. Bake until hot and top is crusty, about 45 minutes.

PER SERVING: Cal. 434, Fat 20g (Sat. 7g), Chol. 29mg, Fiber 5g, Pro. 12g, Carb. 53g, Sod. 1,044mg

Bacon-Cheddar Muffins

PREP: 10 min. COOK: 20 min. YIELD: 12 muffins COST PER MUFFIN: ¢

- 5 strips bacon
- 1½ cups all-purpose flour
- ½ cup cornmeal
- 2 tsp. baking powder
- ¼ tsp. salt
- ¼ tsp. black pepper
- ½ cup shredded sharp Cheddar cheese
- 1 large egg, beaten
- 1 cup milk
- 3 Tbsp. unsalted butter, melted

1 Preheat oven to 400°F. Line a dozen muffin cups with paper liners and set aside.

2 Cook bacon in large skillet over medium heat, turning often until crisp, about 5 minutes. Transfer to paper towels to drain; reserve 2 Tbsp. bacon fat from pan.

3 Whisk together flour, cornmeal, baking powder, salt and pepper in a large bowl. Then stir cheese into mixture. Beat together egg and milk in a small bowl; stir into dry mixture.

4 Crumble bacon. Add bacon, reserved bacon drippings and melted butter to batter. Fold with rubber spatula until blended. Spoon batter into prepared muffin cups. Bake about 20 minutes, until springy to touch. Let cool for 10 minutes before serving.

PER MUFFIN: Cal. 160, Fat 8g (Sat. 4g), Chol. 40mg, Fiber 1g, Pro. 6g, Carb. 16g, Sod. 358mg

Corn Bread

PREP: 10 min. BAKE: 20 min. COOL: 20 min. SERVES: 8 COST PER SERVING: ¢

- 2 cups yellow cornmeal
- 2 cups all-purpose flour
- ½ cup sugar
- 1 Tbsp. baking powder
- 2 tsp. salt
- 1 stick (½ cup) cold unsalted butter
- 2 cups milk
- 2 large eggs

1 Preheat oven to 425°F. Grease a 13-by-9-inch baking pan.

2 Whisk together cornmeal, flour, sugar, baking powder and salt in a large bowl. Add butter and blend into dry mixture with fingers until mixture is mealy.

3 Whisk together milk and eggs in another bowl. Add to dry mixture and stir with a fork just until liquid is incorporated. Scrape into prepared pan and bake until a toothpick inserted in center comes out clean, about 20 minutes.

4 Cool in pan on a rack for 20 minutes before serving.

PER SERVING:
Cal. 478, Fat 17g (Sat. 9g), Chol. 94mg, Fiber 4g, Pro. 11g, Carb. 71g, Sod. 1,331mg

Cheddar Biscuits

PREP: 25 min.   BAKE: 15 min.   YIELD: 16 small biscuits   COST PER BISCUIT: ¢

- 1½ cups all-purpose flour
- 4 tsp. baking powder
- ½ tsp. baking soda
- ½ tsp. salt
- 1½ cups coarsely shredded Cheddar cheese (about 6 oz.)
- ½ stick (¼ cup) cold unsalted butter, cut into small pieces
- ¾ cup buttermilk

1   Preheat oven to 450°F. Whisk together flour, baking powder, baking soda and salt in a mixing bowl. Cut in cheese and butter with a pastry blender or 2 knives until pieces resemble small peas.

2   Make a well in center of flour mixture and add buttermilk. With a fork, toss gently until mixture is just moistened; dough will be very sticky. Do not over mix.

3   Turn dough out onto a well-floured work surface and knead very lightly once or twice with floured hands, sprinkling dough lightly with enough flour to keep it from sticking. Using floured hands, gently but firmly pat out dough ½ inch thick.

4   Dip a 2-inch biscuit cutter into flour and cut out biscuits, dipping cutter into flour as necessary. Gather scraps and repeat. Transfer biscuits to an ungreased baking sheet and bake until golden brown, 12 to 15 minutes. Serve warm.

PER BISCUIT: Cal. 106, Fat 6g (Sat. 4g), Chol. 20mg, Fiber 0g, Pro. 4g, Carb. 9g, Sod. 268mg

MAKE BIGGER BISCUITS

If you prefer larger biscuits, pat out the dough ¾ inch thick and cut with a 3-inch cutter. You'll get about 8 biscuits.

Tennessee Buttermilk Biscuits

PREP: 15 min. CHILL: 30 min. BAKE: 14 min. YIELD: 2 doz. COST PER SERVING: ¢

- 4½ cups plain cake flour (not self-rising), plus more for work surface
- 2 Tbsp. sugar
- 1½ Tbsp. baking powder
- 1 tsp. salt
- 6 Tbsp. cold unsalted butter, cut into pieces
- 6 Tbsp. vegetable shortening
- 1½ cups buttermilk

1 In a large bowl, toss together cake flour, sugar, baking powder and salt. Add butter and shortening and cut in with 2 knives or a pastry blender until mixture resembles coarse meal. Pour buttermilk into mixture and stir just until dough comes together in a ball. Knead briefly on a flour-covered work surface, return to bowl, cover and chill for 30 minutes to let dough rest.

2 Move an oven rack to top third of oven. Preheat oven to 450°F. Lightly flour work surface and roll out dough to ½-inch thick. Using a 1½-inch biscuit cutter, cut out as many biscuits as possible and then transfer to a large, ungreased baking sheet, spacing biscuits about 1 inch apart. Gather remaining scraps of dough and reroll into a ball. Roll out dough and cut as many biscuits as possible.

3 Bake dough on rack in upper third of oven for 12 minutes, rotate pan and bake for about 2 minutes, until biscuits are golden. Serve warm with plenty of softened butter.

PER BISCUIT: Cal. 157, Fat 6g (Sat. 3g), Chol. 9mg, Fiber 0g, Pro. 3g, Carb. 22g, Sod. 180mg

Peanut Butter–Chocolate Cookie Ice Cream Cake page 81

Fallen Chocolate Soufflé Cake page 91

Upside-Down Pear and Apple Tart page 76

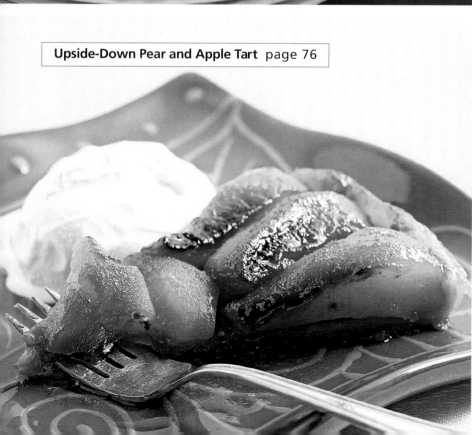

Georgia Peach Cobbler page 84

Berry and Cream Cups page 86

Desserts

Dessert, no matter how small, is always exciting, and here we have 18 delightful treats that will satisfy your sweet tooth. Savor summer's bounty with a **Blueberry Lattice Deep-Dish Pie** (page 77), celebrate a birthday with **Carrot Cupcakes** (page 87) or impress guests with our **Lavish Lemon Cake** (page 94). Whether you're a chocolate lover or a fan of fruit, we've got something here to scratch your itch.

SIMPLE STRAWBERRY NAPOLEON

An impressive—and easy—way to end a summer meal, this luscious dessert has only 4 ingredients and takes just minutes to put together!

1 Cut 2 sheets of puff pastry in half. Bake 3 of the squares at 400°F for 18 minutes, or until they are puffed and golden. Let cool completely.

2 Whip together 1 cup crème fraîche and 2 Tbsp. confectioners' sugar in a medium bowl until fluffy. Hull and slice 8 oz. fresh strawberries.

3 Lay one piece puff pastry on a work surface. Spread with half of crème fraîche mixture and half of strawberries; repeat layers with a second piece of puff pastry and remaining crème fraîche mixture and strawberries. Top with a third piece of puff pastry. Dust with confectioners' sugar. Serves 4.

Caramel Turtle Tart

PREP: **25 min.** COOK: **20 min.** CHILL: **30 min.** SERVES: **12** COST PER SERVING: **$**

- 1 package dough for a 9-inch pie shell, thawed
- 2½ cups sugar
- ¾ cup water
- 1½ Tbsp. light corn syrup
- ¾ cup plus 1 Tbsp. heavy cream
- 1 cup coarsely chopped pecans
- ½ tsp. vanilla extract
- 1 oz. semisweet chocolate, finely chopped
- ½ tsp. vegetable oil
- Sweetened Whipped Cream, for serving (optional)

1 Fit pie shell dough into a 9-inch tart pan with a removable bottom. Preheat oven and bake tart shell according to package directions. Let shell cool completely.

2 Combine sugar, water and corn syrup in a small, heavy saucepan. Bring to a boil over medium-high heat without stirring. Continue cooking without disturbing until mixture turns golden (about 15 minutes). Reduce heat to low, carefully drizzle in ¾ cup cream and then stir until smooth. Stir pecans and vanilla extract into caramel mixture and then scrape into prepared tart shell. Chill for at least 30 minutes (or up to 2 days).

3 Place chocolate, remaining 1 Tbsp. cream and vegetable oil in a small microwavable bowl; heat mixture for 2 minutes at medium (50%) power. Stir until smooth. (If it doesn't melt after 2 minutes, microwave in additional 30-second intervals until smooth.)

4 Transfer chilled tart to a serving platter. Scrape melted chocolate into a corner of a small, sturdy plastic bag. Cut off tip and drizzle chocolate on top of tart. Chill again until ready to serve.

PER SERVING: Cal. 365, Fat 19g (Sat. 6g), Chol. 22mg, Fiber 2g, Pro. 2g, Carb. 49g, Sod. 87mg

SWEETENED WHIPPED CREAM

Beat 1 cup heavy cream in a deep bowl with an electric mixer on medium-high speed until it begins to thicken. Add 2 Tbsp. confectioners' sugar and ½ tsp. vanilla extract and beat just until cream forms soft peaks. Yields 2¼ cups.

PER SERVING (ABOUT 3 TBSP.): Cal. 74, Fat 7g (Sat. 5g), Chol. 27mg, Fiber 0g, Pro. 0g, Carb. 2g, Sod. 8mg

Upside-Down Pear and Apple Tart

PREP: 15 min.   COOK: 50 min.   COOK: 20 min.   SERVES: 8   COST PER SERVING: $

- 1 package frozen puff pastry
- 3 Gala apples
- 3 Bartlett pears
- 2 Tbsp. fresh lemon juice
- 5 Tbsp. unsalted butter
- ⅔ cup sugar
- 1 Tbsp. grated fresh ginger
- ½ tsp. salt
- Vanilla ice cream, optional

1 Preheat oven to 400°F. Remove puff pastry from freezer to defrost.

2 Peel, core and quarter apples and pears. Toss with lemon juice.

3 Cream together butter, sugar, ginger and salt in a bowl. Spread mixture on bottom and sides of a 10-inch round thick-bottomed flameproof and ovenproof baking pan or skillet.

4 Place apple and pear wedges skinned side down in alternating concentric circles on top of butter mixture. (Cut any extra pieces to fill in gaps and pack tightly; tart will shrink when baked.)

5 Place pan over medium-high heat and cook fruit for about 20 minutes or until butter mixture begins to brown. Remove pan from heat; cool slightly.

6 On a floured surface, lightly roll out one sheet of puff pastry and cut out a 10-inch round using base of a 10-inch tart pan or a stencil. Using a fork, poke holes all over pastry. Place pastry on top of fruit in pan, tucking in outer edges to seal.

7 Bake tart until pastry turns golden, about 30 minutes.

8 Remove tart from oven and let cool for about 20 minutes. While pan is still warm, remove tart: Place a plate over top of pan and, holding plate firmly, invert pan quickly onto plate; remove pan. Serve warm with vanilla ice cream, if desired.

PER SERVING: Cal. 374, Fat 20g (Sat. 6g), Chol. 19mg, Fiber 3g, Pro. 3g, Carb. 50g, Sod. 151mg

Blueberry Lattice Deep-Dish Pie

PREP: 30 min. BAKE: 20 min. SERVES: 10 COST PER SERVING: $

The crust:

- 2 cups all-purpose flour
- ½ tsp. salt
- 10 Tbsp. cold unsalted butter, cut up
- 5 to 6 Tbsp. ice water

The filling:

- 2½ lb. fresh blueberries (10 cups)
- 2 cups sugar
- ⅓ cup cornstarch
- White from 1 large egg, beaten
- 2 tsp. sanding sugar

Make crust:

1 Combine flour and salt in a food processor; pulse to blend. Add butter and process until mixture resembles coarse crumbs (do not overblend). Add 5 Tbsp. ice water and process; add more if needed, 1 tsp. at a time, until dough just begins coming together on the blade. Turn dough onto a work surface and knead briefly to form a ball. Pat into 2 squares; wrap them separately in plastic and chill.

2 Invert a 9 by 9 by 2-inch glass or enameled baking dish onto a sheet of parchment. Trace around perimeter of pan. Reserve pan and parchment.

Make filling:

3 Combine blueberries, sugar and cornstarch in a large, heavy saucepan; mix well. Cook over medium-high heat until mixture boils. Reduce heat and simmer, stirring occasionally, until mixture is thick and no longer cloudy, about 5 minutes. Pour into baking dish.

4 Preheat oven to 425°F. Roll out 1 piece of dough on a lightly floured work surface to an 8-by-10-inch rectangle. With a fluted pastry wheel or pizza wheel, cut dough into 1-inch-wide strips. Lay parchment on a large baking sheet. Arrange strips in a row in one direction within pencil outline. Trim edges so strips fit inside lines. Repeat with remaining piece of dough and perpendicularly weave in to make a lattice; trim ends. Brush with beaten egg white; sprinkle with sanding sugar. Bake for 20 minutes; reduce oven temperature to 325°F and bake 15 to 20 minutes more, until golden and crisp.

5 Place baked lattice on top of filling; trim edges so it fits inside dish and on top of fruit.

PER SERVING: Cal. 421, Fat 12g (Sat. 7g), Chol. 31mg, Fiber 4g, Pro. 4g, Carb. 78g, Sod. 129mg

Lots o' Lemon Meringue Pie

PREP: 45 min. BAKE: 30 min. COOL: 2 hr. SERVES: 8 COST PER SERVING: ¢

- 1 disc Classic Pie Pastry (recipe below)
- 1¾ cups sugar
- 1/3 cup cornstarch
- ¼ tsp. salt
- Water
- 4 large eggs, separated
- ¼ cup fresh lemon juice
- 1 Tbsp. grated fresh lemon zest
- 1 Tbsp. unsalted butter
- ¼ tsp. cream of tartar

1 Preheat oven to 425°F. Roll out dough into an 11-to-12-inch round and fit into a 9-inch pie pan. Crimp edge. Prick along bottom of shell with a fork. Refrigerate for 10 minutes.

2 Line pastry shell with foil and fill with pie weights. Bake for 6 minutes, remove foil and bake for 10 minutes longer, until pastry is crisp. Let cool.

3 Reduce oven temperature to 350°F. Make filling: In a medium saucepan, whisk 1¼ cups sugar with cornstarch and salt. Whisk in 1½ cups water and bring to a boil. Boil for 1 minute. In a small bowl, whisk 1 cup of hot mixture into egg yolks. Whisk that mixture into saucepan. Whisk in lemon juice and lemon peel; bring to a boil. Cook, whisking, for 1 minute. Whisk in butter. Pour lemon filling into pie shell.

4 Make meringue: Using an electric mixer, beat egg whites and cream of tartar at medium speed to soft peaks. Gradually beat in remaining ½ cup sugar, 1 Tbsp. at a time. Beat until stiff.

5 Spread meringue on filling up to crust edge; form peaks.

6 Bake pie until meringue is golden at its peaks, 8 to 10 minutes. Let cool; refrigerate for 2 to 3 hours until cold.

PER SERVING: Cal. 422, Fat 16g (Sat. 7g), Chol. 127mg, Fiber 1g, Pro. 5g, Carb. 67g, Sod. 178mg

CLASSIC PIE PASTRY

Stir together 1½ cups flour and ¼ tsp. salt. Cut in ¼ cup cold shortening and 4 Tbsp. cold unsalted butter until crumbly. Mix in 3 Tbsp. ice water with a fork. Knead once or twice. If dough is too dry to form a ball, sprinkle with 1 Tbsp. water and knead. Form dough into a disc, wrap in wax paper and refrigerate for 20 minutes. (Pastry can be frozen for up to 1 month.) Yields 1 (9-inch) pie shell.

PER SERVING: Cal. 181, Fat 12g (Sat. 5g), Chol. 16mg, Fiber 1g, Pro. 2g, Carb. 16g, Sod. 73mg

Fresh Plum Lattice Pie

Lots o' Lemon Meringue Pie

Sour Cherry–Almond Crumb Pie

Fresh Plum Lattice Pie

PREP: 35 min. BAKE: 1 hr. COOL: 1 hr. SERVES: 8 COST PER SERVING: **$$**

- 2½ lb. firm plums, quartered and pitted (about 6 cups)
- 1¼ cups sugar
- 3 Tbsp. quick-cooking tapioca
- 1 Tbsp. fresh lemon juice
- 2 discs Classic Pie Pastry (recipe p. 78)
- 1½ Tbsp. unsalted butter

1 Move rack to lower third of oven. Preheat oven to 400°F. Mix plums, sugar, tapioca and lemon juice well in a bowl.

2 Roll out 1 disc of dough into an 11- to-12-inch round and fit gently into a 9-inch pie pan. Crimp edge.

3 Spoon filling into pie shell. Dot with butter; set aside.

4 Roll out remaining piece of dough into a 12-inch round. Cut into 12 strips, each ¾ inch wide. Lay 6 dough strips evenly over pie, using longer strips in center and shorter ones on sides. Fold back every other strip to its midway point. Place a new strip at a 90-degree angle over unfolded strips. Unfold folded strips, crossing new one. Then fold back alternate strips and place another new strip parallel to first one. Continue weaving in this fashion so that you have 3 strips on this half of pie. Then weave crust on other half of pie in same fashion.

5 Place pie on baking sheet and bake until filling is bubbly and crust is golden, about 1 hour. Transfer to a rack to cool for about 1 hour before serving.

PER SERVING: Cal. 593, Fat 27g (Sat. 12g), Chol. 37mg, Fiber 3g, Pro. 6g, Carb. 85g, Sod. 146mg

Sour Cherry–Almond Crumb Pie

PREP: 25 min. BAKE: 1 hr. SERVES: 8 COST PER SERVING: **$**

- 6 cups fresh sour cherries, pitted
- 1 cup sugar
- 3 Tbsp. cornstarch
- 1 Tbsp. fresh lemon juice
- 1 disc Classic Pie Pastry (recipe p. 78)
- ½ cup all-purpose flour
- 4 Tbsp. unsalted butter
- ¼ cup almond paste
- ¼ cup packed brown sugar
- Pinch of salt
- ⅓ cup sliced almonds

1 Preheat oven to 400°F. Mix cherries, sugar, cornstarch and lemon juice in a bowl.

2 Roll out dough into an 11- to-12-inch round and fit into a 9-inch pie pan. Crimp edge.

3 Crumble flour, butter, almond paste, brown sugar and salt in a bowl until blended. Add almonds and toss.

4 Spoon filling into pie shell; sprinkle with topping. Bake until topping is golden, about 1 hour. Let cool.

PER SERVING: Cal. 508, Fat 23g (Sat. 9g), Chol. 31mg, Fiber 4g, Pro. 6g, Carb. 74g, Sod. 114mg

Peanut Butter–Chocolate Cookie Ice Cream Cake

PREP: 10 min. **FREEZE:** 3 hr. **SERVES:** 16 **COST PER SERVING:** ¢

- **1 (9 oz.) package chocolate wafer cookies**
- **¾ cup natural peanut butter**
- **1 pint each vanilla chocolate-chip, chocolate and vanilla fudge ice cream**
- **1 cup heavy cream**
- **½ cup confectioners' sugar**
- **1 oz. semisweet chocolate, grated (optional)**

1 Line a 9-inch square baking dish with two 24-inch sheets of plastic wrap, allowing excess to hang over sides. Arrange 9 cookies flat side down in bottom of pan and 3 cookies standing up against each side.

2 Warm peanut butter in microwave for 30 seconds; drizzle ¼ cup on cookies in pan. Spoon chocolate-chip ice cream on top and cover with 8 cookies. Repeat layering twice with remaining peanut butter, each remaining pint of ice cream and remaining cookies. Cover with overhanging plastic wrap and press down to compress layers. Cover with a second sheet of plastic wrap and freeze for at least 3 hours and up to 1 week.

3 To unmold, dip pan into warm water, unwrap cake and invert a platter on top. Flip cake over and remove pan and wrap. Return cake to freezer.

4 Whip cream and confectioners' sugar until stiff. Spread on cake and sprinkle with chocolate, if desired.

PER SERVING: Cal. 353, Fat 22g (Sat. 10g), Chol. 61mg, Fiber 2g, Pro. 7g, Carb. 32g, Sod. 164mg

Rhubarb-and-Strawberry Crisp

PREP: 15 min. BAKE: 45 min. SERVES: 6 COST PER SERVING: **$$$**

- 1 lb. rhubarb, chopped
- 2 pints strawberries, hulled and halved lengthwise, large strawberries quartered
- ½ tsp. vanilla extract
- ¾ cup granulated sugar
- 3 Tbsp. cornstarch
- 1 cup rolled oats
- 1 cup firmly packed brown sugar
- ¾ cup all-purpose flour
- ½ tsp. cinnamon
- ¼ tsp. salt
- ⅛ tsp. ground nutmeg
- 1 stick (¼ lb.) cold unsalted butter, cut into cubes
- 1 cup walnuts, chopped
- 1 pint vanilla ice cream

1 Preheat oven to 375°F. Grease a 2-quart shallow ceramic or glass baking dish.

2 Combine rhubarb, strawberries and vanilla in a large bowl. Whisk together granulated sugar and cornstarch in a small bowl. Stir into fruit mixture. Pour fruit into prepared baking dish.

3 Combine oats, brown sugar, flour, cinnamon, salt and nutmeg in a bowl. Pinch butter into dry ingredients with your fingers until combined. Stir in nuts. Spread topping evenly on fruit.

4 Place dish on foil-lined baking sheet and bake crisp until topping is golden brown and fruit is bubbling, about 45 minutes. Let cool for 10 minutes. Serve warm with vanilla ice cream.

PER SERVING: Cal. 787, Fat 36g (Sat. 15g), Chol. 91mg, Fiber 7g, Pro. 10g, Carb. 111g, Sod. 125mg

Peach and Blackberry Crumble

PREP: 15 min.   COOK: 30 min.   SERVES: 6   COST PER SERVING: **$$**

- 1¼ lb. peaches, peeled, pitted and sliced, or 1 (16 oz.) bag frozen peach slices, thawed
- 2 (5.6 oz.) containers fresh blackberries, picked over
- Finely grated peel of 1 lemon
- ⅓ cup plus ½ cup light brown sugar
- 2 Tbsp. cornstarch
- ½ cup flour
- ½ cup blanched, almonds, finely sliced, chopped or ground
- ¼ tsp. salt
- 6 Tbsp. butter, cut into pieces

1 Preheat oven to 400°F. Grease an 8-inch square baking dish.

2 Combine peaches, blackberries, lemon peel, ⅓ cup sugar and cornstarch in a medium bowl. Distribute evenly in baking dish.

3 In a medium bowl, mix together flour, almonds, salt and remaining ½ cup brown sugar. Cut in butter with a pastry blender or two knives until mixture resembles coarse meal. Sprinkle in an even layer over fruit.

4 Set baking dish onto a foil-lined baking sheet to catch any juice that might bubble over. Bake until golden and bubbling, about 30 minutes. Let cool for 10 minutes.

PER SERVING: Cal. 391, Fat 18g (Sat. 8g), Chol. 31mg, Fiber 6g, Pro. 5g, Carb. 56g, Sod. 101mg

SPEED UP THE PREP

Pulse the dry ingredients in a food processor until the nuts are ground. Add the butter and pulse to a coarse meal texture.

Georgia Peach Cobbler

PREP: **20** min.   BAKE: **45** min.   COOL: **15** min.   SERVES: **10**   COST PER SERVING: **$**

The filling:

- 4 lb. ripe, fresh peaches, peeled, pitted and sliced
- ¾ cup packed light brown sugar
- 2 Tbsp. all-purpose flour
- ¼ tsp. salt

The topping:

- 2¼ cups all-purpose flour
- ½ cup granulated sugar
- 2 tsp. baking powder
- ¼ tsp. salt
- 1 stick cold unsalted butter, cut into pieces
- 1¼ cups low-fat buttermilk
- 1 large egg

1 Preheat oven to 400°F. Butter a 9-by-13-inch pan. Put peach slices in pan. Sprinkle with brown sugar, 2 Tbsp. flour and ¼ tsp. salt. Stir gently to incorporate into peaches. Bake for 20 minutes (mixture should begin to boil).

2 While peaches are cooking, make the topping: Toss together flour, granulated sugar, baking powder and salt in a bowl. Add butter pieces and cut into dry mixture with two knives or a pastry blender. Beat the buttermilk and egg together with a fork, then stir into dry mixture until dough comes together into a ball.

3 Remove peaches from oven. Drop dollops of dough in a single layer on top of peaches with a soupspoon. (There will be enough dough for about 20 dollops.) Bake for 20 to 25 minutes, until topping is golden and springy to touch. Let cobbler cool for at least 15 minutes before serving.

PER SERVING: Cal. 373, Fat 11g (Sat. 6g), Chol. 48mg, Fiber 4g, Pro. 6g, Carb. 67g, Sod. 218mg

TOP IT OFF

Nothing pairs better with peach cobbler than a scoop of vanilla ice cream! Making your own isn't difficult, it just takes a little time.

1 Scrape seeds from 2 halved vanilla beans with a knife into a 5- or 6-quart saucepan. Add beans. Add 2 quarts milk and ¼ tsp. salt; bring to a simmer over medium heat until milk just starts to bubble.

2 Whisk 12 egg yolks, 2¼ cups sugar and 2 cups heavy cream in a large bowl.

3 Gradually whisk 3 cups warm milk into egg mixture. Slowly stir mixture into remaining simmering milk in saucepan. Cook over medium-high heat, stirring, until mixture coats back of spoon, about 10 minutes. Strain into chilled bowl sitting in an ice bath; stir until just warm. Cover and refrigerate until chilled.

4 Spoon mixture into ice-cream maker and freeze according to manufacturer's instructions.

Chocolate-Cherry Bread Pudding

PREP: 15 min.   COOK: 1 hour 10 min.   SERVES: 8   COST PER SERVING: $

- ½ cup unsweetened dried cherries
- ⅓ cup brandy
- 2 cups heavy cream
- 1¾ cups milk
- 1 cup sugar
- ¼ tsp. salt
- 7 oz. bittersweet chocolate, chopped, plus extra for serving
- 4 eggs and 3 egg yolks
- 1 tsp. vanilla extract
- 1 (10 oz.) loaf brioche or challah bread, cut into 1-inch cubes
- Whipped cream, optional

1 Preheat oven to 325°F. Grease a 2-quart baking dish. Cook cherries and brandy in a small saucepan over medium heat until simmering; remove from heat and set aside.

2 Bring cream, milk, ½ cup sugar and salt to a boil in a saucepan. Remove from heat and stir in chocolate to melt.

3 Whisk eggs, yolks and remaining ½ cup sugar. Whisk in one-third of the chocolate mixture slowly and then remaining mixture and vanilla to finish custard.

4 Layer baking dish as follows: one-third of brioche, half the cherries, another one-third brioche, remaining cherries (and brandy) and remaining brioche. Pour custard on top to soak brioche.

5 Place bread pudding dish in a larger dish or pan and pour enough hot water into larger pan to come two-thirds up the sides of pudding dish. Bake until just set and center jiggles slightly, about 1 hour, 10 minutes. Let cool.

6 Spoon pudding into dishes. Top with whipped cream and shaved chocolate, if desired.

PER SERVING: Cal. 711, Fat 12g (Sat. 23g), Chol. 297mg, Fiber 3g, Pro. 12g, Carb. 74g, Sod. 427mg

Berry and Cream Cups

PREP: 5 min. BAKE: 30 min. SERVES: 6 COST PER SERVING: **$$**

- 1 (10 oz.) package frozen puff pastry shells
- 1 pint fresh strawberries, hulled and halved
- 1 (6 oz.) container fresh blackberries or blueberries, picked over
- 1 (6 oz.) container fresh raspberries, picked over
- 3 Tbsp. confectioners' sugar
- 1 Tbsp. fresh lemon juice
- 1 cup heavy cream

1 Preheat oven to 400°F. Place pastry shells onto a parchment-lined baking sheet. Bake until golden brown and raised, 20 to 25 minutes. Remove pastry shell tops and soft pastry below with a fork to form a well. Return bottoms to oven to bake centers, 4 to 5 minutes. (Reserve tops for another use. Shells can be baked 1 day ahead; reheat for 3 to 5 minutes at 375°F).

2 Mix berries with 1 Tbsp. confectioners' sugar and lemon juice. Set aside.

3 Whip cream and remaining 2 Tbsp. sugar with an electric mixer until semi-firm peaks form, 3 to 4 minutes.

4 Fill pastry shells evenly with berries. Top with a heaping spoonful of whipped cream and serve.

PER SERVING: Cal. 389, Fat 28g (Sat. 13g), Chol. 55mg, Fiber 5g, Pro. 5g, Carb. 31g, Sod. 246mg

---

KITCHEN TIP

Use whichever fresh fruits are in season. Plums, peaches and apricots are all good choices.

Carrot Cupcakes

PREP: 10 min. BAKE: 25 min. FROST: 15 min. YIELD: 12 cupcakes COST PER SERVING: ¢

- 1 cup flour
- 1 cup sugar
- 1 tsp. baking powder
- ½ tsp. baking soda
- ½ tsp. cinnamon
- ¼ tsp. salt
- 1 large egg plus 1 large egg white, at room temperature
- ⅓ cup vegetable oil
- 8 oz. carrots (about 3 medium), peeled and coarsely shredded
- 3 cups Vanilla Buttercream (recipe below)
- Chocolate kisses and colored sprinkles (optional)

1 Preheat oven to 350°F. Line a muffin tin with paper liners; set aside.

2 Stir together dry ingredients in a medium bowl. Beat in eggs, oil and carrots with an electric mixer.

3 Spoon batter into prepared cups. Bake for 25 minutes. Let cupcakes cool completely before frosting.

4 Frost and decorate cupcakes as desired.

PER SERVING (1 CUPCAKE): Cal. 408, Fat 26g (Sat. 13g), Chol. 70mg, Fiber 1g, Pro. 3g, Carb. 43g, Sod. 220mg

VANILLA BUTTERCREAM

- 4 egg whites
- 1 cup sugar
- 2½ sticks (10 oz.) cold unsalted butter, cut into cubes
- ¼ tsp. salt
- 1½ tsp. vanilla extract

1 In an electric mixer bowl set over a saucepan of simmering water, whisk egg whites and sugar until sugar is nearly dissolved.

2 Remove bowl from pan. Whip mixture at high speed until stiff. Reduce speed and beat until cool, 5 minutes. (Mixture must be cool before adding butter.)

3 Add cold butter 1 piece at a time at medium-low speed. Beat at high speed until fluffy. Add salt and vanilla and mix at low speed until well blended.

PER SERVING (¼ CUP): Cal. 241, Fat 19g (Sat. 12g), Chol. 52mg, Fiber 0g, Pro. 1g, Carb. 17g, Sod. 69mg

Pretty-in-Pink Strawberry Cake

PREP: **20** min. BAKE: **50** min. COOL: **1** hr. SERVES: **12** COST PER SERVING: **$$**

For cake:

- 2 sticks (½ pound) butter
- 2 cups sugar
- 4 large eggs
- 2 tsp. vanilla extract
- 1 Tbsp. baking powder
- 1 tsp. salt
- ½ tsp. baking soda
- 3 cups all-purpose flour
- 2 cups buttermilk
- 1 pint (8 oz.) strawberries, hulled and chopped

For strawberry buttercream:

- 1 pint sliced berries
- ⅓ cup water
- 4 large egg yolks
- 1½ cups confectioners' sugar
- ½ tsp. salt
- ½ Tbsp. lemon juice
- 4 sticks (1 lb.) butter

For garnish (optional):

- 1 strawberry, cut into a fan

Make cake:

1 Preheat oven to 350°F. Line 2 (9-inch) cake pans with parchment; grease paper.

2 Cream butter and sugar in a medium bowl with an electric mixer on high speed. Reduce speed to medium and beat in eggs one at a time, then beat in vanilla extract, baking powder, salt, and baking soda. Stir in flour and buttermilk alternately with a spatula or wooden spoon. Fold in chopped strawberries. Scrape batter into prepared pans.

3 Bake until a cake tester comes out clean, 45 to 50 minutes.

Make strawberry buttercream:

4 While cakes cool, combine sliced berries and water in a small saucepan over medium-high heat. Bring to a boil, stirring; remove from heat. Whisk yolks and confectioners' sugar together with a fork; stir into strawberry mixture. Stir in salt and cook over low heat, whisking, until temperature reaches 170°F. Remove from the heat and beat in lemon juice; let cool. Beat in butter 2 Tbsp. at a time with an electric mixer on high speed until fluffy. Add a drop of red coloring, if desired.

Assemble cake:

5 Place one cake layer on a platter. Spread ¾ cup buttercream on top with a spatula or wooden spoon. Add top layer and frost cake with remaining buttercream. Garnish with a strawberry fan, if desired.

PER SERVING: Cal. 774, Fat 50g (30g Sat.), Chol. 269mg, Fiber 2g, Pro. 8g, Carb. 76g, Sod. 492mg

KNOW YOUR STRAWBERRIES

Refrigerate strawberries, unwashed, until ready to use. Rinse and hull them right before eating or cooking.

Cultivated strawberries. These strawberries are the ones you see most often at the supermarket. They're sweet and range from 1 to 2 inches in diameter.

Alpine, or wood, strawberries. Sometimes called by their French name, **fraises des bois**, these intensely fragrant and sweet berries are smaller and pointier than the cultivated ones. They can be found at farmers' markets.

Applesauce Cake with Cream Cheese Frosting

PREP: **20 min., plus cooling** BAKE: **40 min.** SERVES: **6** COST PER SERVING: ¢

- 1 cup all-purpose flour
- 1 tsp. baking soda
- 1 tsp. cinnamon
- ½ tsp. ground allspice
- ¼ tsp. salt
- Pinch of ground cloves
- 1 stick (¼ lb.) unsalted butter, softened
- ½ cup light brown sugar
- ½ cup granulated sugar
- 1 large egg, room temperature
- 1 cup applesauce, room temperature
- 1 cup chopped walnuts
- ¾ cup raisins
- 6 oz. cream cheese, softened
- 3 Tbsp. unsalted butter, softened
- ¾ cup confectioners' sugar
- 1 tsp. vanilla extract

1 Preheat oven to 350°F. Butter an 8-inch square metal baking pan and lightly dust with flour, shaking out any excess.

2 Whisk together flour, baking soda, cinnamon, allspice, salt and cloves in a bowl; set aside.

3 Cream butter and sugars in a medium bowl with an electric mixer on high speed until fluffy, about 5 minutes. Add egg and beat well until blended. Mix in applesauce at low speed, then add flour mixture, mixing at low speed until incorporated. Stir in walnuts and raisins. Scrape batter into prepared pan and bake 40 minutes, until cake tester inserted in center comes out clean. Let cake cool completely in pan.

4 Beat cream cheese and butter together in a bowl until smooth. Add sugar and vanilla extract and mix until blended. Spread frosting on cooled cake and cut into 6 pieces.

PER SERVING: Cal. 763, Fat 45g (Sat. 21g), Chol. 123mg, Fiber 3g, Pro. 9g, Carb. 87g, Sod. 416mg

Fallen Chocolate Soufflé Cake

PREP: **30 min.** BAKE: **35 min.** SERVES: **12** COST PER SERVING: **¢**

- 1 lb. semisweet chocolate, chopped
- 2 sticks (½ lb.) unsalted butter
- 10 large eggs, separated
- ¾ cup plus 1 Tbsp. sugar
- Unsweetened cocoa powder, for dusting
- Sweetened Whipped Cream (see recipe, page 74), optional
- 15 raspberries, optional

1 Position rack in middle of oven and preheat oven to 300°F. Butter and flour a 9- or 10-inch springform pan and line bottom with parchment paper.

2 Melt chocolate and butter in a double boiler, whisking until smooth. Remove top pot from heat and let chocolate cool to room temperature.

3 Beat egg yolks and ¾ cup sugar with an electric mixer on medium-high speed until very thick and pale, about 5 minutes.

4 Beat egg whites in a large, clean bowl with clean beaters just until soft peaks form when beaters are lifted. Beat in remaining 1 Tbsp. sugar.

5 Gently fold one-third cooled chocolate mixture into egg yolk mixture with a whisk or rubber spatula. Fold one-third egg whites into batter. Repeat, adding chocolate mixture and egg whites alternately in thirds, until ingredients are combined.

6 Transfer batter to prepared pan. Bake for 30 to 35 minutes, until edges are firm and center is puffed but still a bit jiggly; do not overbake. Transfer to a rack to cool completely.

7 Remove side of pan and dust cake with a thin layer of cocoa powder. Serve with whipped cream and raspberries, if desired.

PER SERVING: Cal. 427, Fat 30g (Sat. 18g), Chol. 221mg, Fiber 2g, Pro. 7g, Carb. 38g, Sod. 61mg

PERFECT PEAKS

Egg whites will not form peaks if there is any fat or water in the bowl. To ensure maximum volume, clean your bowl and beaters with vinegar or lemon juice and dry thoroughly with a clean towel before whipping eggs.

Chocolate-Cherry Cakes

PREP: 30 min., plus cooling time BAKE: 30 min. CHILL FROSTING: 2 hr. SERVES: 8 COST PER SERVING: $

The cake:

- 2 oz. unsweetened chocolate
- 1½ sticks (12 Tbsp.) unsalted butter, softened
- 1½ cups sugar
- 3 large eggs, at room temperature
- ½ cup unsweetened cocoa
- 2 tsp. baking powder
- 1 tsp. pure vanilla extract
- ¼ tsp. salt
- 1¼ cups all-purpose flour
- 2 oz. (1½ cups) fresh cherries, pitted, plus cherries with stems for garnish

The frosting:

- 8 oz. semisweet chocolate, finely chopped
- 2½ cups heavy cream
- 2 Tbsp. confectioners' sugar

Make cake:

1 Microwave unsweetened chocolate in a small microwavable bowl for 2 minutes at medium (50%) power. Stir; cook in 30-second increments until melted. Reserve.

2 Preheat oven to 350°F. Grease a 13-by-9-inch metal cake pan; line it with greased parchment paper.

3 Cream butter and sugar with an electric mixer on high speed until fluffy, about 5 minutes. Beat in eggs, one at a time, beating well after each addition. Add cocoa, baking powder, vanilla extract and salt; mix at low speed until blended. Mix flour in at low speed until just incorporated; mix in reserved chocolate until just incorporated.

4 Batter will be thick. Scrape it into prepared pan and smooth top. Press pitted cherries into surface of batter at 1-inch intervals; bake 25 to 30 minutes, until a toothpick inserted into center comes out clean. (Do not stick pick into a cherry.) Let cake cool for 10 minutes, invert pan onto a tray, then invert cake onto cooling rack; cool completely.

Make frosting:

5 Melt semisweet chocolate in 1 cup of cream in a small saucepan over medium heat; stir until smooth. Scrape into a bowl, then stir in second cup of cream and chill for at least 2 hours. Beat cold chocolate cream with an electric mixer until thick (do not overbeat or mixture may become grainy).

Assemble cakes:

6 Beat ½ cup cream with confectioners' sugar until stiff but not dry. Using a 2½-inch-diameter cookie cutter, cut out 8 rounds of cake; arrange on a platter. Frost cakes, dollop with whipped cream and top with a fresh cherry.

PER SERVING: Cal. 817, Fat 55g (Sat 33g), Chol. 210mg, Fiber 5g, Pro. 9g, Carb. 83g, Sod. 156mg

ALL ABOUT CHERRIES

Cherry season typically runs from June through August, so grab a big bag of these ruby-red fruits when you see them in your favorite grocery store or local farmers' market. Enjoy them with sweet treats, like these Chocolate Cherry Cakes, or try using cherries in savory dishes. Duck, pork tenderloin, lamb and chicken all pair well with fresh summer cherries.

Lavish Lemon Cake

PREP: 25 min.   BAKE: 55 min.   COOL: 1 hr.   SERVES: 12   COST PER SERVING: ¢

Lemon cake:

- 5 large eggs, separated, plus 3 large egg whites
- ½ tsp. cream of tartar
- 2¼ cups cake flour
- 1½ cups sugar
- 1 Tbsp. baking powder
- ½ tsp. salt
- ½ cup vegetable oil
- ½ cup fresh lemon juice
- 1 Tbsp. finely grated fresh lemon zest
- 1 tsp. vanilla extract
- ½ cup water

Marshmallow frosting:

- 1½ cups sugar
- 3 large egg whites
- ¼ tsp. salt
- Pinch cream of tartar
- 1½ tsp. vanilla extract
- Lemon slices, optional

1 Place rack in bottom of oven; preheat oven to 325°F. Set aside an ungreased 10-inch tube pan.

Make lemon cake:

2 Beat egg whites with an electric mixer at medium speed for 1 minute. Add cream of tartar; beat until stiff, 3 to 4 minutes. Sift flour, sugar, baking powder and salt together into a bowl. Make a well in center and add yolks, oil, juice, peel, vanilla extract and ¼ cup water. Whisk liquids; gradually stir in dry ingredients. Fold one-third of egg whites into batter. Fold in remaining whites. Scrape batter into pan.

3 Bake cake until a cake tester inserted in center comes out clean, 50 to 55 minutes. Invert pan; let cool.

Make marshmallow frosting:

4 Bring sugar and ½ cup water to a boil over high heat to dissolve sugar. Then boil to 240°F on a candy thermometer. Beat egg whites, salt and cream of tartar with an electic mixer at medium speed until stiff but moist. Beat hot sugar syrup into mixture. Add vanilla extract; beat until cool.

5 Run a knife around cake; remove pan. Put cake on platter, frost and arrange lemon slices around the side, if desired.

PER SERVING: Cal. 409, Fat 11g (Sat. 2g), Chol. 90mg, Fiber 1g, Pro. 6g, Carb. 72g, Sod. 300mg

GET THE RIGHT GRATER

For extra-fine shavings, use a Microplane® grater. It's ideal for citrus zest, hard cheese, chocolate, coconut, nutmeg, garlic and ginger.

Index